LEADERSHIP GIANTS

Lessons from My Life in Educational Leadership

DR. GUY ALBA

Leadership Giants

ISBN: 978-0-9996297-1-0

First edition: August 2023

Guy D. Alba Ed.D.
9 Candice Court
Johnston, RI 02919
(401) 286-4428
guydalba@gmail.com

COMMUNICATION is what you say and how you say it. CONNECTION IS WHAT THEY HEAR. COMMUNICATION, no matter how well-intentioned, sometimes misses its target completely.

-Tim David

INTRODUCTION

Welcome! Clear expectations are essential to relationships and meaningful human connections. This publication involves reflections on a life well spent as a counselor educator, central administrator, principal, school counselor, and teacher. The first draft was titled, "*No Little Kid Ever Grew up Wanting to Be Assistant Principal.*" That's a quote from a dedicated assistant principal who was serving in his 32nd year at the same inner-city high school. We served together in my first official school administration appointment. He must have been a great lightweight wrestler in his school days because he took that same approach to his work as an administrator. Only Baby-Boomers that are former hockey stars approach educational "battles" with more enthusiasm than former wrestling champions. He threw himself into each situation with little regard for his personal safety or well-being. There will be a few stories from those years that I will share as they become relevant to the topics discussed. I am grateful to Tony for his insights that helped set the tone for my early school administration work.

I changed all of the names in these stories and the numerous others throughout this book. As my reflections unfolded, the narrative expectations changed.

What follows is a somewhat more academic, educational leadership offering that focuses on career development from the counselor and administrator perspective. The stories take the "Textbook Feel" out of the lessons. For twelve years I had the honor of teaching hundreds of graduate school aspiring educational leaders along their personal career journeys.

Professional school counselors and administrators are truly "Leadership Giants!" My "Giant" themes and perspectives were influenced by the inspirational works of John Amaechi, OBE. He wrote a great book called, "The Promises of Giants." It has been described as "...one of the most powerful books ever written about leadership." It includes focus areas that demand intentional, unconditional, persistent, full-time focus for all who have the honor of being Educational Leader Giants. I will mention a few of these "Promises," but it may be helpful to learn a little about Dr. Amaechi. He is a respected organizational psychologist, best-selling New York Times author, and sought-after public speaker.

He was awarded the Order of the British Empire (OBE) for his contributions to charity and sport. He was the first Briton to have a career in the NBA. He was the first openly gay former NBA player. That led to much of his early fame, although he is quick to point out that he didn't earn that fame any more than he earned his six-foot ten-inch height. His jersey hangs in the US Basketball Hall of Fame in Springfield, Massachusetts. I enjoyed seeing his smooth moves on the NBA courts and came to a deeper appreciation of his thinking even more when I learned his back story.

This link provides a peak into his early career. https://vimeo.com/133266894 . He is a "giant" on many levels.

IMPOSTER SYNDROME AND LEADING PEOPLE WHO ARE SMARTER THAN YOU.

Perhaps the first and foremost promise is the one leadership giants make to themselves. This is the promise to view themselves critically, objectively, and compassionately (not cruelly).

I frequently told my graduate students that leader competence begins with leader self-understanding. This requires introspection and the initiative to engage in self-analysis. We may experience "Imposter Syndrome"- The feeling that you are a fraud and undeserving of your place, that you are, in reality, substandard, and that at any second, people will "find out" and "expose" you.

How we act, in dealing with this feeling makes all the difference. Being a teacher often involves helping learners who are smarter than you! The same holds true for principals, counselors, and central office educational leaders. ...Let that sink in for a minute!

Many of my friends went right into teaching after college. I was impressed! That was something I thought was beyond my comfort zone. My fear was that I did not know enough stuff to teach others. I feared I would teach students everything I knew in the first class and then we would be stuck staring at each other. My alternate pathway was to follow my love of sports into the business world. Part of my career in business involved designing athletic shoes. This was a team-oriented, fast-paced, high-fashion, technology-rich field.

It was exciting and almost as much fun as working in education. I taught many school lessons drawing on my business experiences. Even teaching from direct experience did not insulate me from imposter syndrome. Middle school students often have a way of expressing themselves that cuts. I was teaching a lesson about a great experience that had a significant impact on the athletic footwear industry, when a student loudly commented, "This is BORING!" I was hurt, and my first thought was to get defensive and fight back and show the student who was boss! Instead, I took it in and upon reflection I realized that although I was **communicating** the ideas, I was not **connecting** with the student(s).

After a revised follow-up lesson, I solicited feedback. This same very vocal middle schooler commented, "That was better than a trip to Rocky Point (a local amusement park)!" We all had a great laugh at this, and my insecurity was momentarily eased. The laugh came easy to me. There was no insecurity about the content that I was teaching.

The lesson itself involved the creation of brand identification side designs on athletic shoes (e.g., the Nike Swoosh, Converse Chevron and Star, etc.). It turns out that stripes on the sides of athletic shoes, that are deemed to be functional (i.e., add stability to the shoes) cannot be trademarked. Walmart could legally market certain shoes with three stripes on the sides, just like Adidas, with no fear of legal jeopardy. I thought this was a really big deal that my mostly brand-conscious middle schoolers would find exciting, if I just communicated it to them. In reality, without connection and engagement even an exciting message misses the target.

I also remembered who the "boss" is really, and what it means! Being a "boss" or "leader" in educational settings require student success as the ultimate measure of progress. Sometimes those being led or supervised have very diverse interests and talents. Some of the students in this middle-school class did not have fancy sneakers. It was a sore topic to them that obscured the lesson I wanted to share. This situation helped me learn about myself and how I could improve my teaching and my leadership.

Leadership success does not require cruelty, even cruelty to yourself! Success requires a clear, vivid, and explicit vision of your preferred future. In developing this vision, I like the way **Russ Sabella** describes the "Miracle Question" in his presentations and publications on the solution-focused approach.

Here is an example of the Miracle Question. *Suppose you woke up one morning and by some miracle everything you ever wanted, everything good you could ever imagine for yourself, had actually happened - your life had turned out exactly the way you wanted it. Think about it now. • What will you notice around you that let you know that the miracle had happened? • What will you see? • What will you hear? • What will you feel inside yourself? • How would you be different?*

Although the vision is absolutely essential, it must be followed by strategic action.

Leadership giants must take care of mind and body. This includes maintaining balance, healthy nutrition (including hydration!), physical activity, occasional pauses for recuperation, and a good night's sleep.

ONE OF THE BEST GIFTS YOU CAN GIVE SOMEONE IS YOUR UNDIVIDED ATTENTION!

When leaders embrace self-attention, they can give others the attention they deserve. Attention as a leadership giant can be viewed as a weapon. It is a strange weapon in that its absence is what is very likely to wound others. One of the very best gifts you can give someone is your undivided attention. Please note that psychologists have found that if your cell phone is visible to you, even if it is off, your companion is likely to view it as a distraction to your attention. Leaders must be intentional in gifting their undivided attention to others. It should be part of the leaders' job description.

In my work as a consultant for the Small Business Association, I counseled employment managers of most businesses to develop comprehensive job descriptions, but I cautioned against reducing the expected potential of people in these jobs to just these distinct roles.

One small business client was a quaint little craft business called "Beauty and the Beads." In addition to a small selection of finished jewelry, incense, and greeting cards, the owners offered an eclectic collection of beads and charms for customers to create their own jewelry. They held classes and parties for customers to come together and work on their pieces. The classes run by the owner were popular and the sales were strong when she was working in the shop. There was a dramatic downturn when a few of the hired helpers were in charge.

I watched the operation and surveyed a few customers. It turns out that some of the helpers were honest employees, but they did not get along well with the other workers and were dismissive with some of the customers. The personal touch, team spirit and the business' bottom line were suffering. Individuals are NOT job descriptions. They met all of the stated job requirements, but they did not see how important they were to the entire operation. They saw their work as just a part time job for a little extra money. I saw this a school principal.

Teachers and administrators are required to meet certification and licensing standards. They meet the basic job description. The calling of the educational leader is to create teams. Groups of teachers and administrators can become teams only when we unleash the potential. They must see how important they are to each other and to the school community.

In **groups**, the job description may be the endpoint of responsibility. In **teams**, it is only the starting point. Principals need to prioritize opportunities for teachers and counselors to collaborate on team projects and share responsibility. As a central administrator in a large district, I saw the interdependence of the school principals and had some limited success in helping develop principal teams.

Being a principal can be a very lonely job. The best of the best recognized their need to form teams that honor their individual strengths and challenges. Teams of leadership giants progress towards their shared vision by acting with vigilance against their biases. This goes beyond recognition of bias, unconscious or otherwise. It is the behaviors that result from those biases that must be addressed. This can make people very uncomfortable. The concept of "privilege" is often misunderstood and the source of discomfort.

It is an absence of a particular impediment, which means we often don't realize we have these privileges when they are present because their impact only crystallizes with their absence. John Amaechi's bitesize video on white privilege has been viewed over three million times. https://twitter.com/bbcbitesize/status/1290969898517254145?lang=en

People are often innocently unaware of their biases. There is a revealing follow up question I have used in class that helps gain perspectives. After asking what students believe or associate with a particular identity (e.g., a person who is gay, or trans, etc.), give them 90 seconds to say, or jot down what they believe other people associate with those identities. While students' respondents often claimed not to personally harbor negative associations, they found it remarkably easy to *create* a list of them in just 90 seconds.

Recognition of bias is important, but accountability for inappropriate biased behaviors is essential. Leaders must ensure that there are tangible, clearly communicated sanctions for inappropriate behavior even if it forces us to confront or part ways with toxic but otherwise productive people we lead.

These values are required of all courageous educational leadership giants. Comedian **Jon Stewart** said, "If you don't stick to your values when they're being tested, they're not values. They're hobbies." While this commitment to values extend to all leadership roles, different competencies must be developed and focused on special domains within education.

INTEREST IN THE POSSIBLE CAREER DESTINATIONS ADD MEANING TO THE SCHOOL JOURNEY

Educational leadership giants work in three domains: Academics, Behaviors (social and emotional), and Careers. I call them the "A, B, C's" of educational leadership. The last "C," Careers, is a central focal point that is often missed. The valid measure of educational effectiveness is the success of students in their life's work, their CAREERS.

Full disclosure, I taught a graduate course in Career Information to aspiring counseling candidates for over twelve years. An early pioneer in Career Education is Frank Parsons. He is often called the Father of Vocational Guidance. In addition to his early work in counselor education, I identified with his work in school administration.

Why would a school administrator prioritize career information? I saw countless supporting instances, but one had a particularly lasting impact on my thinking. I was serving as an Assistant Principal at an inner-city high school. Part of the duties involved addressing serious behavior problems. I received a call for assistance from the Art teacher. A student was swearing at the teacher and had destroyed classroom materials. I took the student to my office and started the accountability process.

Investigating the incident involved reviewing the student's academic progress in addition to citizenship. I noticed that her marks looked like an EKG, with high grades in some very challenging science courses. She was slumped in a chair in my office with her arms crossed when I asked this 18-year-old high school senior about her plans for the future. She replied, "I have no idea, whatsoever!" I mentioned her good science grades and asked her if she knew anyone, besides me, who loved what they were doing for work. She looked at me with great surprise and said, "you like your job?" I assured her that I loved my job and went back to the original question. She said she didn't know anyone else who really loved their job, but one of her aunts seemed to be enjoying her work as a Certified Nursing Assistant (CNA). She mentioned the great pay, and a few of the nice things she was able to afford. She said she would like to know more about that career field, and planned to look it up when she had the chance.

While she was there, I called a good friend and colleague who was directing the CNA program at our local community college. I told her that I had a student with great potential, who was interested in exploring the CNA program and I requested an appointment for the next morning. I confirmed the time with the student and assured her that she would be available at that time since she was suspended from school during that time.

To be clear, I have never been a big fan of out-of-school suspensions for student misconduct. Something has gone wrong before the suspension that should have been addressed. The student communication network in most schools is very strong and active. One student leader commented to me that "None of my suspensions were 'Shady.'" She explained that they were not out of meanness, and grossly viewed as unfair. It made me feel a little better, but I still hate out-of-school suspensions in general.

Back to my current Art Class student… She attended the meeting at the Community College with the CNA Director and then came to me with her parent for a reinstatement from suspension conference at the school. I was surprised to learn that she had applied and been accepted into the CNA Program upon graduation. We discussed how CNA's make lifesaving and life-improvement decisions and treatment interventions. I advised her to start thinking of herself as a CNA rather than someone who behaves in totally inappropriate and unacceptable ways in her high school classes.

There were other accountability measures taken, but the point is… her behavior changed dramatically. With her new perspectives, she was successful in academics and citizenship. This experience helped me relate to Frank Parson, and other school leaders who insist that their students think about careers in age-appropriate ways. This is so important that I framed many of my educational leadership lessons that follow, in an intentional manner that addresses career education.

Here is a general outline of topics: We start with the importance of valuing the intelligence of all workers and the relationship between work and perceptions of intelligence. This appreciation is applied to specific guidelines to help educators unleash the power of school and business/community partnerships. There have been dramatic changes over the years in the dynamics of the relationships between the school and business community.

We examine historical perspectives and the impact of immigration on career development. Several influential theories and models are reviewed to help educational leaders work strategically to address this changing landscape.

The Solution-Focused Approach, and in particular, the advice of **Russ Sabella** has major implications for the successful application of these theories and models. It also guides our approach to the authentic assessment of student learning and the ways we serve and celebrate diverse populations of students. Particular attention is given to work in service to students with disABILITIES. We finish with a brief commentary on expectations of "loyalty."

VALUING THE INTELLIGENCE OF ALL WORKERS.

Mike Rose, a wonderful and generous educator, shared his thinking in numerous publications on valuing the intelligence of all workers and the work they do. His ideas shaped my perspectives over the years. I used his books and articles in many of my classes, and I gratefully acknowledge his influence in these ideas.

One of my first jobs as a young adult was in a newspaper production facility. I was a "Flyboy" in a union shop, working under the watchful eye of my brother-in-law, **Billy Riordan**. He was the union vice-president and has always been one of my heroes. The work was very physical. It involved carrying engraved printing plates to the presses, moving 1,200-pound rolls of print paper to the press reels, cleaning up the core rolls, and the entire work area. The ink in the air turned everything and everyone in the non-air-conditioned press room dingy. At the end of a shift all the "Flyboys" were exhausted and filthy.

Prior to cleaning up, if I had to go out of the facility, people on the street would often look away or give me a little extra space on the sidewalk. I remembered that. The more experienced, higher ranking "Pressmen" enjoyed a little better workday and conditions. The pay was wonderful and the pathway from "Flyboy" to "Pressman" was relatively clear. I seriously considered dropping out of college to pursue this career field, and I continue to respect the skills and talents involved in newspaper production. I think of it every time I pick up a paper. It impacted the way I relate to Mike Rose's work.

Rose suggests that many professions are honored and widely respected for the intelligence of their workers. Brain surgeons, rocket scientists, etc., are acknowledged as "smart." We want to extend this notion about intelligence up and down the ladder of occupational status. The mind and body connections are clearly evident in the power of physical work to engage people.

There is a long history of people making assumptions not only about the moral benefits of physical work but also about the intellectual capacity of the working class in general, and urban youth in particular. History is rich with tales of "Hard Physical Labor" assigned to prisoners. Physical work and those that perform it are often seen as less intelligent. This valuation extends to views on abstraction.

Abstraction is the essence of mathematics; the source of its power is its independence from the material world. …this fact has been converted in our intellectual history into a series of judgments about the worth and status of kinds of mathematics…. the more applied and materialized the mathematics is, the less intellectually substantial it is often perceived.

Historically, Western culture has tended to oppose technical skill to reflection, applied or practical pursuits to theoretical or "pure" inquiry, the physical to the conceptual.

In reality, we learn powerful things about the world not only by reflecting on it but also by acting on it – and what we learn through action can well move us to the contemplative.

How do we make decisions about who's smart and who isn't? How does the work someone does feed into that judgment? What are the effects of such judgments on our sense of who we are and what we can do? These are our guiding questions.

Most cultures make judgments about competence in the domains that matter to them. Unfortunately, we in the U.S. tend to label entire categories of work and the people associated with them in ways that generalize, erase cognitive variability, and diminish whole traditions of human activity. We order, rank, and place at steps upon a ladder rather than appreciating an abundant and varied cognitive terrain.

We need to look at a job being done and think: What is going on here? How is it learned? What enables it to happen? What in this moment does it mean to be smart? To prepare students, they need to experience "rigorous" learning experiences that prepare them for smart work. We ask, what is rigorous learning? Asking the right questions is a special pathway to learning.

One of my favorite teachers, **Charles Mojkowski**, shared that gift with me and so many others. He advises educational leaders to keep students engaged. We must provide learning experiences outside school as a formal part of their programs of study. It may sound counterintuitive, but we keep students in school by acknowledging their need to *leave* school to learn. This requires strategic planning that starts with how we plan to assess progress. There are an amazing number of tools to assess and audit the quality of a school.

Consistent focus areas are the "rigor" of the curriculum, the quality of instruction, the sophistication of the assessments, and student performance on those assessments. In all of these areas, student voices need to be heard! They play an important role in comprehensive assessments for learning. I appreciate the way Mojkowski envisions student questions that should be included in ***their*** assessments on the quality of learning and ***their*** learning environments.

They fall under the following headings: Relationships, Relevance, Choice, Challenge, Authenticity, Application, Play, Practice, Time, and Timing. It would be nice if there was nice acronym for this, but we have enough of those in education. For ***relationships***, students might ask: "Do my teachers, and others who serve as my teachers know about me and my interests and talents?" "Do my teachers help me form relationships with adults and peers who serve as models, mentors, and coaches concerning my career interests?" "Do my teachers help me build relationships in the school community and in out-of-school communities?"

For ***relevance,*** students might ask: "Do I find what the school is teaching to be relevant to my interests, including my career interests?" "Do my teachers help me understand how my learning and work contribute to my community and to the world?" For ***choice,*** "Do I have real choices about what, when, and how I will learn and demonstrate my competence?" "Do my teachers help me make good choices about my learning and work?" For ***challenge,*** "Do I feel challenged in my learning and work?" "Am I addressing real-world, high, and meaningful standards of excellence?" For ***authenticity*** "Is the learning and work I do regarded as significant outside school by my communities of practice and by experts, family members, and employers?" "Does the community recognize the value of my work?"

For ***application*** "Do I have opportunities to apply what I am learning in real-world settings and contexts?" "Do I have opportunities to contribute to solving the problems my community and the world are facing?" For ***play*** "Do I have opportunities to explore – and to make mistakes and learn from them – without being branded as a failure?" "Do my teachers coach me in tinkering, experimenting and speculating?" For ***practice*** "Do I have opportunities to engage in deep and sustained practice of the skills I need to learn?" "Do my teachers guide me in practicing correctly?"

As the old saying goes, ***practice makes perfect***. It is important to note that practice makes perfect only if we practice **perfectly**. Practicing mistakes is counterproductive. For ***time*** "Do I have sufficient time to learn at my own pace?" Having goals that are time-bound are important. We must strike a thoughtful, strategic balance in applying time constraints to student learning. Is seat time more important than mastery learning? I suggest that the answer is a resounding NO! There is an art to addressing this challenge in school settings.

Mojowski and the Big Picture Schools team continue to do ground-breaking work in this area. They facilitate student learning out of the standard sequence. While we often hear teachers say, "May I have your attention?" To students, it is just as important to have their teachers pay this kind of attention to their students. Teachers and counselors have expectations too. Understanding the dynamic between principals, counselors, and teachers is essential to success.

The Mojowski-influenced guiding questions follow the same pattern as the student questions above. Again, the focus is on Relationships, Relevance, Choice, Challenge, Authenticity, Application, Play, Practice, Time, and Timing. You will note that many of these questions are identical to those posed by students to their schools. This is clearly intentional! For ***relationships***, counselors and teachers might ask: "Does my principal know about me and my interests and talents?" Does the professional development program help me build relationships for learning in my school and in communities of practice outside my school?

For ***relevance,*** they might ask: "Do I find that what the school is offering me for professional development is aligned with my personal learning plan and career interests?" "Does my principal help me to see how my specific professional development experiences contribute to what we need to accomplish for our students?" For ***choice,*** "Do I have real choices about what, when, and how I will learn and demonstrate my competence?" For ***challenge,*** "Do I feel challenged in my learning and work?" "Am I addressing real-world, high, and meaningful standards of excellence?"

For ***authenticity*** "Do my communities of practice regard the learning I do as significant?" For ***application*** "Do I have opportunities to apply what I am learning in my classroom or school with my students?" For ***play*** "Do I have opportunities to explore – and to make mistakes and learn from them – without being branded as a failure?"

For ***practice*** "Do I have opportunities to engage in deep and sustained practice of the skills I need to learn?" "Does my school provide expert practitioners to coach me in my classroom and school?" For ***time*** "Do I have sufficient time to learn at my own pace?" For ***timing,*** "Can I pursue my learning out of the standard sequence?

Counselor, teacher, and administrator competence begins with self-understanding. These insights allow us to form the relationships to learn and teach the essential skill of valuing the intelligence of all workers and students and appreciating them as people.

UNLEASHING THE POWER OF SCHOOL AND BUSINESS/COMMUNITY PARTNERSHIPS

A long-past generation spoke of the three "**R's**" of education, as "**R**eading," "w**R**iting," and "a**R**ithmetic." The new three "**R's**" are **R**igor, **R**elevance, and **R**elationships. You can see how the student questions start us on the road to understanding these objectives. It is that third "R," relationships, that facilitates the other two.

Human relationships are at the heart of what we do as educational leaders. Harvard University conducted a seventy-five year, thirty-million-dollar study on The Meaning of Life. It was human connection that they concluded was the meaning. To connect and develop meaningful relationships we must listen and notice. I often describe intentional noticing as a super-power of effective educational leaders.

It was my great fortune to meet an expert on human connections, **Tim David.** When we first met, he was performing a magic act at a local Rotary Club. He was absolutely amazing! In our follow up conversations, he explained that the real key to his "magic" was his ability to connect with his audience. He went on to publishing fame and guest appearances on national and international stages.

One of my favorite articles that Tim published is titled, "Why Doesn't Anybody Listen?" With his trademark humor, and insightful commentary he suggests that if we want to influence others and really listen, we should "Never make them feel stupid!" I added the underline to the "feel" in this quote to emphasize its importance.

When someone is confronted with facts that are contradictory to their actions, they have two choices, admit that they're wrong (and therefore admit that their actions were stupid), or ignore the facts and justify their actions. I and most others prefer the second option. People are more likely to believe their own words over anything someone else is saying. Guiding them to solving their own challenges is much more effective.

Tim gives the example of influencing a person to quit smoking. Instead of preaching or threatening about the factual dangers, you may want to ask the smoker, "Why do you want to quit?" As the person responds and reflects, anything they say is going to be much more powerful than anything you could possibly say. Educational leaders would do well to heed Tim's advice, the "Cardinal Law of Persuasion" is "Never Make Them Feel Stupid!"

As the famous saying goes, "people will forget what you said and often, even what you did... but they will always remember how you made them feel." How does our work make us feel? How do we feel about people who do repetitive work that some people mistakenly refer to as unskilled work? There is really no such thing.

We take this essential competency for nurturing relationships to our discussion on unleashing the power of school and business/community partnerships. Schools should prepare students for success in their continuous learning plans and in their careers. People outside of education frequently talk of "failing schools." Unacceptably low-test scores are presented as evidence of these "failures."

The attacks have the same impact as making people feel stupid, and the lack of persuasion is very predictable. What is needed is for leaders to… TAKE A CLOSER LOOK, and intentionally listen to each other! No relationships are more impactful for success in education than those interactions between schools and businesses. I use the term "businesses" as a general descriptor that includes community organizations. My strong personal connection to this aspect of leadership developed through my individual career journey that straddles both worlds.

I graduated from college with a degree in Business Administration and experienced some success in the corporate world in senior management positions, and in local business enterprises. Business was fun, for me. I was fortunate to work with some outstanding leaders. My love for sports and athletics added to my excitement in a range of assignments.

As I mentioned earlier, I got to design athletic shoes. I even owned and operated my own fitness center and karate studio before I realized my lifelong dream to become a teacher. I took these business perspectives into my career in education.

For those of us who have served in substitute teaching assignments for any length of time, it is likely that some life-changing experiences were involved. One encounter stays with me and impacted my sense of urgency on the need to bring the worlds of business and education closer.

I was assigned to substitute for a high school "Business Teacher." The first class was "Business Math." Prior to going into class, I was nervous about the level of rigor that was needed. I had used math related elements of Physics, Calculus, Chemistry, and Statistics in designing athletic shoes. I anticipated that a course called "Business Math" was at a level that exceeded "AP Calculus BC."

Imagine my shock, when I saw the text and lesson plan was limited to fourth and fifth grade arithmetic! The administrator explained to me that "Business Math" and other courses titled "Business ________," were designed for students that were not in the "college prep." track. They were designated as less able academically. I had never experienced this "lower track" designation as a student in the private schools I attended.

In addition to the "Business Math" experience, my next class was "Office Simulation." I saw a classroom full of female students with headphones on typing away on electric typewriters. When I asked what they were doing, the supervisor said they were taking dictation, "just like in a real business office." I really needed the work as a substitute teacher, so rather than objecting to these misguided perspectives, I decided to take every opportunity to change the "Business Education" paradigm in whatever limited capacity I could.

When I was assigned to my own permanent Business Teacher Position, I was excited about the opportunity to change things. This was encouraged by my first school principal. When I asked about the curriculum, and other expectations, he said, "Weren't you in business for many years? Do pretty much what you want." "Let me know the outcomes you expect for the students."

My current teacher friends will find that hard to believe. There is so much unfortunate micro-management of instruction, in far too many classrooms. My first classroom had been vacant for over a year, in a building erected in 1929. There were some electric typewriters (and two manuals!) in a corner and mix and match chairs and desks. Some were likely hold-overs from the original construction.

Most of the better furniture had been scavenged by other teaches for their own rooms. Even the shades on some of the windows of this basement level room had been trimmed to let in the glaring afternoon light. The few textbooks were over twenty years old. I knew I had to get help from outside of the school. Like most teachers, I had a part-time job. I was a fitness instructor at the corporate fitness center of a large insurance company. They were distinguished by their unwavering dedication to the highest ETHICAL standards.

As an exercise instructor, I had access to people at all levels of the organization, including the highest-level executives. When you are holding weights above someone's head or leading them in a strenuous exercise routine, they pay particular attention to you.

I was excited about my new Business Teacher position, and I told them about it. These kind folks asked me, "How can we help you?" You should understand that most large companies are bombarded by requests for donations. My insurance company executives were surprised when I said what I wanted was for them to look at what I was teaching my students and make sure it reflected the latest business methods and competencies. I wanted an on-going relationship between my school and this corporation. They responded in amazing ways, helping me to strategically plan and act in a comprehensive manner to benefit my students.

I had them come to visit my school and classroom. Although I never asked them for a donation of any kind, they saw many needs that matched their own community service objectives and donated hundreds of thousands of dollars in materials and in-kind resources. They also made it clear that they did not see their role as "providing for the school, what the taxpayers were obliged to provide." Public schools are funded through a combination of local, state, and federal dollars, with the federal government covering less than 10 percent.

My school principal was thrilled with this arrangement and even the district superintendent met with the company executives to express appreciation. I saw that educators cannot and should not work in isolation. Unleashing the power of school and business partnerships was essential to success. This theme has been a major influence on my life, including my professional research. I studied the limited body of research on the most effective school and business partnerships I could find, in the hopes of developing a facilitation model and an evaluation tool. As I describe these ideas, I encourage educators to think about the relationships in their school communities that have benefited students, and how we can increase and replicate their impact.

To be good partners with business, educators must recognize some of the basic differences between businesses and schools that impact our relationships.

PARTNERSHIPS - OPPORTUNITY COST AND RETURN ON INVESTMENT (ROI)

Classic marketing strategy in business directs practitioners to point out the benefits of their product to their prospect. The more the prospect perceives personal benefits, the more likely they are to buy it.

Opportunity Cost is what you give up in order to get something else. In business, very often the costs of business potentials are measured against the potential benefits. If the results do not suggest a positive outcome, or the ROI is deemed insufficient, the project is not pursued.

This is very different from the school setting, especially the public-school setting. The public-school educational leaders' mandate is to serve all students regardless of the costs. Some students cost two or three times as much to serve as others. Return on investment is not a consideration!

Those who must administer public school finances often do not have control over the expenditures. Collective Bargaining Agreements and savage inequalities in school financing make school budgeting and financial planning a very different process from the methods used by successful businesses.

Ethical, successful businesses must be nimble in their innovative approaches to serving their customers. They often innovate even when things are going exceptionally well. Schools often do not have this same degree of flexibility. There is a long history of resistance to change even in the face of dramatic changes in students' needs.

Donald Siegel suggests that U.S. school systems are where American companies were 15 to 20 years ago, when business leaders discovered that they could no longer compete in an international marketplace. For the first time, education leaders confront an equally formidable challenge; They must determine how to meet higher performance expectations, not just for some but all students (Siegel, 2000). This situation has not substantially improved in the years since Siegel's thoughtful comments.

PARTNERSHIPS – EVALUATION

A partnership is a **relationship** between the people within separate institutions. Partnership, like change, is a process, not an event. Partnership goals often change over time from the needs for affiliation, moving to the establishment of mutual responsibilities and benefits, to increased commitment (U.S. Department of Education Office of Educational Research and Improvement (OERI), 1993).

Evaluation is an essential part of the overall partnership planning process. By closely linking management, planning, and evaluation, a partnership may find it easier and quicker to actively learn and adopt strategies and practices that improve effectiveness (National Association of Partners in Education (NAPE), Inc., 1997) (Alba, 2020).

Evaluation informs the planning process, management, and partnership improvement. Criteria, and indicators in the areas of partnership assessment and evaluation focus on five main areas: 1. Mission, 2. Planning and development, 3. Program design and management, 4. Implementation process, and 5. Evaluation (NAPE, 1993) (Alba, 2014, 2016, 2020).

PARTNERSHIP CONFIGURATIONS

The following school and business partnership configurations are often mentioned in the research: the Project Driven Model, the Adopt-a-School Model, and the Reform Model.

As a school principal, I continued to embrace opportunities for educators to unleash the power of school and business partnerships. Here is an example to illustrate the most common type of school and business partnership – the Project Driven Partnership.

My school was located in the inner city. To open up the school to ideas from the community, we created a Distinguished Guest Reader (DGR) Program. Ethical community leaders were invited to visit the school for a one-time session to read a story to a class. The invitations were sent by the teachers, and the readers were prepared with a brief tutorial on how to do a read-aloud with an elementary school class.

They were also provided a text unless they had one of their own that was vetted by the teacher. After the class sessions, I met with each Reader to debrief and offer them an opportunity to stay in touch with the school in the future. One Distinguished Guest Reader, the Chief of Police, had an exceptionally wonderful time. He was enthusiastic about staying in touch and asked about what else he could do to support our school. My request for a relationship with this organization was similar to my request for a relationship with the insurance company mentioned previously. But this relationship had a much more focused mission.

We wanted to address a social problem, student perceptions of the role of police in society. The Chief agreed to send members of his force to co-teach a class once a week, with the teacher. I worked with the sixth-grade social studies classroom teacher and administered a pretest essay on student perceptions of the role of police in society. They had some fun with this assignment, and mentioned things like, bullying criminals and family members, punishing speeders, eating donuts, etc. I shared them with the Police Chief. He wasn't known for his great sense of humor, but he recognized the need.

For the next six weeks police officers and senior staff visited the school to hold classes and develop a relationship with students. At the end of this time period, the students redid their essays on the role of police in society. They overwhelmingly stated that police were here to "protect and serve." They made lasting contacts. The teachers loved having police officers coming into the building on a regular basis. Some strong relationships were created there as well.

When I showed the revised essays to the Chief of Police, he was very gratified. He posted them up in his office for everyone to see! This was a successful project-driven partnership. Not all project-driven partnerships have to be this involved.

Another example was a partnership to improve student attendance. We invited a sister-team (**Julie Zito** and **Lisa Costentino**) business owners of a gourmet pastry chain to be guest readers. When they offered to stay in touch with our school on a limited basis, we targeted improving student attendance. They offered gourmet cupcakes to students who improved their attendance over a semester. These were really great cupcakes! Although it cannot be completely attributed to the cupcake prize, student attendance improved substantially, and the thank-you notes from students to the company were displayed prominently at the pastry shops. As you can see from these examples, Project-driven partnerships are usually formed to address specific academic or social problems. Project-driven partnerships in general have relatively short-term focus objectives that may be isolated from the rest of the school activities.

The relationship between the insurance company and my school that I described earlier, is an example of an Adopt-a-School Model. The Adopt-a-School model usually involves a single company and a single school to provide resources and volunteers to support school activities. Attention is normally paid to symptoms rather than to causes of critical student needs. It is normally beyond the scope of such a partnership to address the root causes of barriers to student success. Although Project-based partnerships sometimes evolve into Adopt-a-School relationships this is <u>not</u> a measure of partnership success.

Reform-Model partnerships focus on systemic change. They try to find ways to change the learning and teaching environment by expanding the responsibilities and roles of students, educators, and the organizational and management structures within schools, districts, and nationally. They are also focused on developing proficiency model assessment tools. Some of the larger educational assessment and reform organizations include specific, intentional lobbying on a national level for legislation efforts supporting education.

A notable Reform-Model partnership initiative resulted in support by senior level federal government officials for school counselors to "Own the Turf" of college and career success. This call to action was supported by federal incentives.

PARTNERSHIPS – ASSESSMENT

My research into the successful school and business partnerships revealed creative, student-centered relationships that had two main common characteristics. First, they were focused on student learning rather than money. The second characteristic was a comprehensive on-going assessment of the partnerships. Simple assessments embraced by educators and business leaders most often involve five major steps: 1. Needs Assessment (Vision), 2. Resource Assessment and Development, 3. Goals and Objectives, 4. Partnership Management, and 5. Documentation and Evaluation. Here is a brief description of these steps.

1. *Vision and Mission* – Educational leaders document what learning outcomes they want to see in place for students at a given time in the future and the reasons why. This forms their base of accountability. Business and educational leaders agree on a concise statement of the broad purpose for the existence of their partnership and how it complements their mutual goals and vision.
2. *Resource Assessment and Development* – The educational leaders explore and develop human, material, and financial resources to turn their vision into reality. It is not the private sector business partner's role or duty to provide financial resources to schools, especially public schools. If it is within the scope of the partnership mission, all partners participate in identifying and/or securing resources.
3. *Goals and Objectives* - The partners develop and document broad statements of desired, measurable, time-bound, teaching, learning, and business goals.
4. *Partnership Management* – The partnership team establishes management procedures that assure partnership com-

pliance with board of education policies regarding health, safety, and participant activities clearly. The team defines the roles and participation guidelines for all business personnel who will be working with students.
5. *Documentation and Evaluation* – A member of the partnership team is directly responsible for documenting and reporting on partnership activities. Evaluation results must be reviewed by the partnership team, approved for release, and reported, as appropriate to the entire learning community.

Educational leaders will continue to feel isolated, overwhelmed, and frustrated with their lack of sufficient learning resources unless they learn to embrace the diverse elements of the business world. Similarly, business leaders will continue to take great pains, and expense, in searching for workers who "Know the right stuff" when they graduate from school.

Taking a closer look at schools and developing partnership relationships for learning, not funding has the power to address issues of equity and adequacy in education. Schools and businesses are different. While we have reviewed ideas about nurturing relationships that address and, in some cases, celebrate these differences, we have a long way to go in addressing diverse populations of students in our schools.

A brief historical review will help understanding.

HISTORICAL PERSPECTIVES AND CURRENT ISSUES OF EQUITY

My first school assignment as principal was in a very familiar place. It was less than a block from my father's barbershop. From the school playground, I could see the roof of the house where I grew up. The neighborhood had changed quite a bit. In my childhood most of the residents were hardworking second and third generation people of Irish, Italian, and Armenian descent.

Now there was a rich mixture of people, many of Hispanic origins. I put up a very large world map in the foyer of the school under a sign that read "Where in The World Are You From?". Pins from every corner of the globe represented our students. Over thirty-nine different languages were spoken in students' homes. The sense of pride was real. It was NOT a melting pot. Too much of the good stuff gets stuck to the edges of a melting pot. This was a smorgasbord of different cultures, with proud traditions. Over ninety-five percent of the students received free or reduced-price meals. Among the numerous challenges associated with poverty, negative expectations can be persistently harmful.

We have a longstanding shameful tendency in America to attribute all sorts of pathologies to the poor. Writing in the mid-nineteenth century, the authors of a report from the Boston School Committee bemoaned the "undisciplined, uninstructed... inveterate forwardness and obstinacy" of their working-class and immigrant students. There was much talk in the Boston Report and elsewhere about teaching the poor "self-control," "discipline," "earnestness" and "planning for the future." Sound familiar?

Along these same historical lines, in 1917 Robert Yerkes responded to the need for large group, quick, mental tests. While Yerkes believed that the tests measured native intelligence, later findings revealed that education, training, and acculturation played an important role in performance. Yerkes also became a prominent figure in the eugenics movement, which advocated for harsh immigration restrictions in order to combat what he referred to as "race deterioration." These findings were used to support the idea of genetic differences between 'races.'

Carl Brigham, one of Yerkes' colleagues, using a genetic explanation of the data proposed the racial superiority of the Nordic people (from Northern Europe). Similarly, it was argued that the average scores from the different national groups reflected innate racial differences. These widely held beliefs had some tragic results.

One was the Immigration Restriction Act (1924). The Immigration Act of 1924, or Johnson–Reed Act, including the Asian Exclusion Act and National Origins Act (Pub. L. 68–139, 43 Stat. 153, enacted May 26, 1924), prevented immigration from Asia and set quotas on the number of immigrants from Eastern and Southern Europe.

There was an interesting facet to these quotas. Instead of using current immigration data, this Act went back to the US Population in 1890 (over 30 years prior to the Act) to set the quotas. Immigration from southern and Eastern Europe was relatively low before this date. Following Eugenics fears the 1924 law makers wanted to guard against race deterioration from the current crop of immigrants. They were fearful. Some of these attitudes persist.

There is no good evidence to support the view that differences in IQ scores are due to genetic differences. There is also a lack of any clear operational definition of intelligence, which obviously undermines any line of argument. Similarly, the concept of 'race' defies definition, which is why we should perhaps argue that 'race' is more a **political** construct rather than a **biological** one.

My grandparents were immigrants to the United States. It took great courage to take this leap of faith for a better life. Both of my grandfathers started businesses. One ran a barbershop and the other opened and ran ice cream shops. This is not unusual for that time and the trend has continued.

The report, "New American Fortune 500 in 2022: The Largest American Companies and Their Immigrant Roots," found that 43.8%, or 219 companies, in this year's Fortune 500 list were founded by immigrants or their children. According to a report released by the Fiscal Policy Institute, immigrants are "twice as likely to start a business as the native-born population." More specifically, about 22 percent of businesses in 2017 were owned by immigrants and 17 percent employed at least one immigrant employee.

There are a number of persistent myths that feed the fear of immigrants. The Cato Institute's Alex Nowrasteh, drawing on years of research and debate, counters common myths against immigration with nonpartisan facts in the report *The Most Common Arguments Against Immigration and Why They're Wrong*. The Corporation supports the Cato

Institute's immigration program where Nowrasteh is director of immigration studies and the Herbert A. Stiefel Center for Trade Policy Studies. Here are a few of their findings:

IMMIGRATION MYTHS VS. FACTS

- **MYTH: IMMIGRANTS ARE TAKING OVER**
  FACT: Immigrants actually only account for 13.5% of the total U.S. population, which is in line with historical norms
- **MYTH: IMMIGRANTS ARE ALL MEXICAN**
  FACT: 30% of immigrants come from Asia, and currently more are coming from China than Mexico
- **MYTH: IMMIGRANTS DON'T WORK**
  FACT: 72.5% of immigrants believe hard work is how you succeed in America and are responsible for half of the total U.S. labor force growth over the last decade
- **MYTH: IMMIGRANTS DON'T HELP THE ECONOMY**
  FACT: Immigrant-owned businesses with employees have an average of 11 employees
- **MYTH: IMMIGRANTS TAKE AMERICAN JOBS**
  FACT: 7.6% of immigrants were self-employed compared to 5.6% of native-born Americans and they founded more than 40% of Fortune 500 companies
- **MYTH: IMMIGRANTS AREN'T EDUCATED**
  FACT: Recent immigrants are more likely to have college degrees than native-born Americans and are more likely to have advanced degrees

DIVERSE POPULATIONS AND ACCESS TO HIGHER EDUCATION

Equity and adequacy issues in transitions to higher education have come a long way due in part to some historical Reform-Model partnerships. For over 120 years, the College Board has played a major role in helping students make successful transitions to higher education. At its founding in 1900, the

College Board was organized to help high school students make a successful transition to higher education. At that time, the handful of colleges that formed the membership association known as the College Entrance Examination Board sought to simplify the application process for students and for those colleges' admission offices.

With the College Board's revolutionary development of common entrance examinations—later known as the SAT® Program or Scholastic Aptitude Tests—students could apply to several institutions without having to sit for entrance examinations at each one. The new assessments also had another democratizing benefit: individuals could provide evidence of their credentials without regard to their family backgrounds and despite inconsistent grading systems and curriculum standards throughout the nation's high schools.

SUPPORTING RESILIENCE BY LOOKING DEEPER
THE $10,000 POM-POM

In my work in the inner city, I saw firsthand that some poor and immigrant families are devastated by violence, uprooting, substance abuse, food insecurity, and lack of clothing.
Children are terribly affected. But some families hold together with iron-willed determination and instill values and habits of mind that middle-class families strive for. There's as much variability among the poor as in any group, and we must keep that fact squarely in our sights, for we easily slip into one-dimensional generalities about them. And one more fact, <u>an awful childhood wreaks damage, but is not destiny.</u>

Poverty can have unexpected impacts on students in school. Educational leaders must consistently look beyond behavioral challenges to investigate causes and intervene. I had a high school student who was a very talented basketball player. His attendance was unacceptable and seemed to follow a pattern.

He had a connection with the basketball coach, so we met together as a team to discuss the attendance issue. Once trust was established, in a tearful revelation, it was discovered that the student had one set of clothes. On laundry day he had no clean clothes to wear to school. That challenge was resolved at that point with a relatively easy solution. A well-stocked clothes closet was established and made available to all in the school and in the community. Many community sponsors and the students themselves contributed.

How many other students have similar challenges that are solved in one setting but are sorely needed in others?

Looking deeper helped me in another memorable situation. One of my high schools had a rule against students wearing hats while in the building. This was a districtwide policy. As I patrolled the corridors and the lunchroom, when I spotted someone wearing a hat, just a nod and a point to my head was enough to get students to remove their hats. No muss, no fuss, no drama… until there was!

A student was sitting in the cafeteria with his friends, calmly eating his lunch wearing his hat. As I came by and made my normal signal reminder to remove his hat, Ronny just looked away and continued to eat. I knew Ronny from his middle school days to the present. He was a great kid who had a history of angry outbursts when embarrassed. I came closer to the table and asked Ronny to please remove his hat. He looked down and simply replied, No. The other students at the table responded with a collective "OOOOOO."

I had a good reputation as a strict, but never mean administrator, and compliance with my direct requests were commonly respected. Ronny's lunchmates knew something bad might be brewing! I was surprised and a little embarrassed by Ronny's "No." I took a quick five-second pause and asked Ronny to take a few minutes and come to see me in my office right after lunch. The hat stayed put! When he came to the office, I said, "Ronny, you must have a very good reason for being disrespectful... what is it?" He said that his cousin cut his hair last night and it was a mess. I asked to see it and discovered that Ronny was being kind in describing it as a "mess." He said that he had an appointment after school to have it fixed. I gave Ronny a pass with one of my school business cards that gave him permission to wear his hat for the rest of the day.

If anyone asked, he could show the card and leave the hat on. In reflecting on the situation, forcing Ronny to remove his hat in the cafeteria would likely have exposed him to ridicule and embarrassment. His likely reactions would have been unpleasant and dangerous.

Cafeteria violence is in a special category that should be avoided at all costs. Looking deeper is a wonderful leadership competency. My judgement was impacted by classroom workshop lessons from **Professor Ralph Montella**. He held up a pom-pom from a hat and asked the class to guess what it represented. He went on to explain that this pom-pom represented a $10,000 settlement reached by his school district. A student was wearing a hat in a school building when he was stopped by a staff member who ordered him to remove it. When the student refused, the staff member snatched the hat from his head and sent him on his way.

In the aftermath it was discovered that the student was wearing this head covering for religious reasons and was carrying a permission pass. He and his family were deeply offended by the actions of the staff member and pressed charges against the district. They were awarded $10,000 in damages. Professor Montella kept the pom-pom from the hat as a visual aid to help encourage educators to show respect, kindness, and patience in looking deeper into student behaviors. Sharing knowledge is important.

THEORIES ADDRESSING THE HIERARCHY OF NEEDS FROM SOLUTION-FOCUSED PERSPECTIVES.

SHARING THE KNOWLEDGE

We see these lessons from recent and past history, but often, in an effort to show the value they are adding to their organizations, educational leaders attempt to re-solve challenges rather than building, improving, and crediting. I find it helpful to review select counseling and administrative theories to add perspective. Theories can help the inexperienced by serving as "road maps" that suggest directions and help ensure they will be effective.

Theories can also help more experienced leaders by facilitating their integration of self and external knowledge. We start with a "first things first" approach of Abraham Maslow. He was a humanistic psychologist best known for his developmental theory of human motivation. Basic human needs must be met before academic learning can take place.

RELATIONSHIPS ARE ESSENTIAL TO SCHOOL SAFETY

One of my greatest frustrations was the amount of time I spent as a school principal keeping people safe from harm.

Some estimates suggest that over 500,000 kids bring a weapon to school every day. I participated in numerous school safety seminars, workshops, and panel discussions with school, law enforcement, public safety, and security experts.

Great strides have been made in technology tools and policies designed to improve safety. Some schools actually have facial recognition technology that identifies everyone entering the building and some systems take the temperature of people entering. Visitors and individuals with high temperatures receive further appropriate attention.

I have also observed metal detectors, bullet proof glass, advanced locking systems, and audio/visual systems that monitor school facilities. In discussions with the experts, they consistently mention <u>human connections</u> as a leading factor in safer school environments. In situations where students had a trusted adult and understood the limits of confidentiality school tragedies of epic proportions have been avoided.

Two situations come to mind from my own school principal experiences. One involves a student with a gun in school, and the other with a machete. Our administration team received a tip that a student at our high school was in possession of a gun. An exhaustive search of the school was unsuccessful.

Finally, a person of interest, an 18-year-old high school senior, was taken to the principal's office to be interviewed. Eric was an imposing figure. He was well over 6 feet tall with a voice like Jason Beghe, the actor who plays Sgt. Hank Voight on the TV show Chicago PD. The actor's distinctive voice is partly due to an accident.

Eric embraced his own booming raspy speech as part of his image. I knew Eric from his squeaky-voiced middle school days. Another administrator was leading the questioning, with Eric giving an occasional grunt in reply to repeated requests for information. Frustration was growing. At that point, Eric pointed at me and said, I only talk to him! When the other's left, Eric looked me in the eye and said, "I know where the gun is…Can you keep it secret?" I said, thank you and reminded him about the limits of confidentiality. It was a discussion we had a few times over our time together. It was then that he reached into the waistband of his baggy pants and drew the weapon out.

I do not know very much about handguns, but I couldn't believe how large this weapon was. It seemed like slow motion as the handle and the long gun barrel emerged. He put it on my desk, and I immediately removed it. At that point Eric put his head on my desk and promptly fell asleep. I certainly was not sleepy at that point! Later we discovered that this was not the first time Eric came to school with a weapon. He had a reputation among other students of occasionally "being strapped" (in possession of a gun or other weapon).

In another case in a later principal assignment, I was doing cafeteria duty (Four hundred students in a lunchroom designed for three hundred twenty-five). Some school principals prefer to delegate cafeteria duty to others, rather than take this substantial chunk of time from their other duties. I have found the cafeteria at lunch time to be one of the best places to take the pulse of the building.

Making eye contact with each student for at least the second time of the day (*greeting students as they enter school is something that I enjoyed*) and exchanging a word or two is important for principals. In this case, it averted a tragedy. Two students approached me in the cafeteria and asked if they could tell me something in private that would stay confidential. I reminded them of the limits of confidentiality, and they proceeded to tell me that "Julio has a knife."

There were several students named Julio, so they gave a better description. They said, "You know Julio, the kid with the Mohawk haircut." Of course, I knew Julio. He had been through recent trauma and drama. Julio had a physical condition that caused him to have seizures. The last time it happened, he was at the bus stop, with many student witnesses. Most were kind and supportive as I quickly got him the medical attention he needed. A few misguided individuals decided to tease Julio about the incident. He reacted violently to this, and severely injured one of them. All were held accountable, and Julio was allowed to transfer to another nearby school at his parent's request.

Now he was trespassing at the back of the school cafeteria. I directed the two students who came to me to smile and enter the cafeteria serving line and wave, as though everything was normal. I walked toward Julio and smiled at him, but he ran towards the exit. I followed and collaborated with the school-based Police Officer to detain him. A search resulted in the discovery of a knife with a twelve-inch blade. I don't know how he was running with this knife in his pants, but he was pretty quick. His feud with those that taunted him was not over. He planned to take it to the next level. The intervention of those two students who came to a trusted adult, the principal, in the cafeteria, helped avert another potential tragedy.

Julio's knife on the hood of a Police Car

These are not isolated incidents. Intentionally nurturing human connections is essential to student success, and educational leader satisfaction. Student safety is a foundational need that is required prior to self-actualization. A comprehensive, strategic effort is required. Fortunately, there are approaches that are very helpful.

SOLUTION-FOCUSED APPROACH
SKI TOWARDS THE PATHWAYS... NOT THE TREES!

I rejoiced in the times when I could get to the next levels and support students' progress and achieve their personal higher-level goals. I found the "solution-focused" theory, as presented by **Russ Sabella**, a life-changing approach that crossed all the past theoretical perspectives. Solution-focused practitioners focus more on solution-talk than on problem-talk.

There is a limited place in solution-focused conversation to talk about problems. While leaders using a problem-solving approach listen for factors that cause or maintain the problem, solution-focused leaders listen for factors that point toward progress or solutions. Giving people the opportunity to talk about their problems is respectful and an important aspect to building the relationship and understanding their problems. This problem focus should not be extensive and should change in a relatively short amount of time to solution talk.

One of my graduate students in the Counseling training program, was an air traffic controller. He described his job in solution-focused terms. He said he communicated successful flight paths to pilots rather than describing in detail the locations of other traffic. Similarly, Simon Sinek suggests that skiers on forest slopes must concentrate on the pathways between the trees rather than focusing all their attention on the trees. Intentionally taking this approach to our educational leadership helps professionally and personally. This has far-reaching implications.

Small Victories

THE "HALF-CAP CEREMONY" AND EARLY WARNING SYSTEM

The Solution-focused approach includes appropriate appreciation of small victories. One relatively small victory for high school students can have a major impact on their futures and on their school communities. Most high schools require students to earn credits towards graduation. When students earn all their required credits for promotion by the end of their sophomore year, they are 80% more likely to graduate on time than their over-aged, under-credited peers. They are clearly halfway there!

To recognize this accomplishment some school leaders have established a "***Half-Cap Ceremony***." They honor the students with a graduation-like mini-ceremony. Graphics often include one-half traditional graduation caps used in programs and even a few actual apparel items. It is a fun celebration that has been used in Chicago, Denver, and Providence. It deserves to

be extended and adopted as a districtwide policy in more settings. The Half-Cap also helps those students who were close to achieving this honor to see exactly what they need to do to get back on track. Denver posted an outstanding "How To" Guide to the Half Cap. See below:
https://studylib.net/doc/6911663/half-cap-cermonies-how-to

I was interviewed by a radio personality on his talk show regarding the "Half-Cap" Ceremony at my school. Initially the host suggested that this effort might be a "Thank you for participating...Everyone gets a trophy... event!" Once he and the listeners heard the data and results, they saw the value and potential.

Awareness of what is needed must be followed up by thoughtful, comprehensive actions. To accomplish this, some high school leaders establish an ***Early Warning System*** (EWS). They budget and schedule tutoring that students access in an exceptionally timely manner. Rather than waiting until the end of a semester or course, the EWS kicks in within weeks of the first signs of falling behind in a course. Teachers, administrators, counselors, and even students themselves can self-refer for these services. Of course, this is tailored to meet the needs of the school, but the preparation and values of the best EWS programs I have experienced are very consistent.

These Half-Cap and Early Warning Systems are concrete examples of small victory celebrations and actions taken by educational leader giants who are taking a solution-focused approach. This approach extends in positive ways to a wide range of human connection needs.

MENTAL HEALTH BASIC FIRST AID

Personal and professional needs are enmeshed like threads in a fabric. Early in my work life I got to design athletic shoes. Attention to the smallest details of the shoe components was required. Even the threads of the fabrics we used in some shoes had to be accurately twisted and then woven into materials meeting specifications that eventually helped athletes to succeed.

It may be over-ambitious to think that a "thread" could cause success, but I know that failure of those materials could harm performance dramatically. Thinking about some of these smaller, "thread" victories helped me to focus on the granular details needed in education and their roles in the fabric of life.

An overwhelming consideration is mental health. Leadership giants need a level of competence to address mental health crisis situations they are likely to face. Personally, I have intervened in numerous situations involving people with mental illness. It left me very anxious to improve my knowledge in these areas.

Additionally, some well-loved family members have addressed a wide range of mental health issues and the quality of support they have received makes me angry. I decided to learn more about the basic, solution-focused approaches to improving mental health and intervention strategies in mental health crisis situations. There are a number of ideas that help leaders to intervene in a timely research-based manner similar to the way a physical first aid class helps intervention in many cases of physical trauma.

Mental health includes emotional, psychological, and social well-being. It affects how people think, feel, and act. It also helps determine how they handle stress, relate to others, and make choices. There are many great courses and training programs that can help leaders gain essential mental health first aid competencies. The National Council for Mental Wellbeing offers outstanding tools. Their "Mental Health First Aid" programs are comprehensive efforts that are taught with fidelity. Successful completion leads to certifications at various levels. I completed the certified instructor training for Youth Mental Health First Aid and found it useful in a number of crisis situations.

There are numerous other mental health first aid trainings that offer useful techniques to help educational leaders intervene in a crisis. The level of skills is similar to the American Red Cross Cardiopulmonary resuscitation (CPR), First Aid, and defibrillator trainings. With widespread CPR training, most of us would know how to help if we saw someone having a heart attack. We would Check for responsiveness, Call 9-1-1, and begin forceful chest compressions at a rate of 100 per minute. If a defibrillator is available, they are easy to use with minimal training.

Unfortunately, I had to use this training. CPR and first aid training is far more common than mental health first aid, but the numbers are rising. Through just the National Council for Mental Wellbeing Mental Health First Aid programs, an estimated 2.6 million people are trained to help their peers, neighbors, colleagues, and friends.

We must recognize that suicide is the second leading cause of death among individuals between the ages of 10 and 34. To be clear, prompt intervention before a mental health challenge turns into a crisis is essential. There are different action plans for mental health first aid to guide interventions. These plans are intended to provide timely, research-based interventions for non-medical crisis situations. Medical supersedes mental. The "ALGEE" plan is very effective. It is not a linear process that follows a strict order of operations. Assessment occurs in all phases. Here is the ALGEE plan:

- **A**ssess for risk of suicide or harm.
- **L**isten nonjudgmentally.
- **G**ive reassurance and information.
- **E**ncourage appropriate professional help.
- **E**ncourage self-help and other support strategies.

The "**A**" and "**L**" of this plan involves Assessing Approaching, Assisting. In Non-Crisis situations, to listen non-judgmentally:

- Don't interrupt; Don't force - use "I" statements (no blame or labeling) it's about them not you! {avoid statements like "When I was your age..."}
- Pay attention to verbal and non-verbal cues [eyes, body, comfort, you may want to sit at an angle from the student, walk together, don't fidget]
- Remember what was said – follow up – be consistent.
- Rephrase, re-cap
- Cultural Considerations → respect the individual and their experiences; Don't make broad assumptions; maintain neutrality; be mindful of language and expressions; recognize potential barriers.
- In assessing for risk of suicide or harm, consider the following:
    - Suicide Attempt is a self-injurious act committed with at least some intent to die, as a result of the act. Any "non-zero" intent to die – does not have to be 100% Intent and behavior must be linked; there does not have to be any injury or harm, just the potential for injury or harm (e.g., gun failing to fire); A suicide attempt begins with the first act (example: first pill swallowed or scratch with a knife.)
    - In 2019 in my home state, Rhode Island, 294 teens ages 13-19 were admitted to the emergency room after a suicide attempt, nearly double the number in 2015 which was 156 (72% female; 28% male)
    - In 2019 174 teens between ages of 13-19, were hospitalized, nearly double the number in 2014 which was 95. Recent data suggests these trends continue.

    - Youth threatened or injured by a peer are 2.5 times more likely to report suicidal thoughts. They are 3.3 times more likely to report suicidal behavior than non-victimized peers.
    - Warning Signs of Suicide (a person who is suicidal generally gives many clues and warnings regarding their suicidal intentions. Alertness to these cries for help may prevention suicidal behavior.)
- There are also important signs that a young person may be suicidal:
    - Talking, writing, or posting on social media about death, dying, or suicide.
    - Threatening to hurt or kill themself.
    - Seeking access to pills, weapons, or other means.
    - Expressing hopelessness, no reason for living or having no sense of purpose in life.
    - Having rage, anger or seeking revenge.
    - Acting recklessly or engaging in risky activities, seemingly without thinking.
    - Feeling trapped.
    - Increasing alcohol or drug use.
    - Withdrawing from friends, family, or society.
    - Having a dramatic change in mood.
    - Sleeping all the time or being unable to sleep.
    - Being anxious or agitated.
    - Giving away prized possessions.
- Assessing for the risk of suicide or harm involves asking the right questions, such as:
    - Have you wished you were dead or wished you could go to sleep and not wake up?
    - **Are you thinking about killing yourself?" If the answer is, "Yes," then…**Have you decided how and when you would kill yourself?" Have you taken any steps to secure the things you would need?
    - Have you ever done anything, started to do anything, or prepared to do anything to end your

life? If yes, ask: How long ago did you do any of these? (Over a year ago? Between 3 months and a year ago? Within the last 3 months?)
    - Keep in mind that while a higher level of planning means higher risk, a lower level of planning does not mean there is no risk.
- Have you been using alcohol or other drugs?
- Have you had family, friends or heroes die by suicide?

The "**G**" of this plan involves giving reassurance and information. In Non-Crisis situations, to feel ***with***, not ***for*** the individual consider the following:

- When people feel understood it helps them recover; Give hopeful statements; Give practical help suggestions; stay with the person and let them know that you will remain; give academic info. if indicated; acknowledge limits of what you can do.
- Things to Avoid → don't make promises you can't keep; don't give unsolicited advice [did the youth ask for your advice?]; don't dismiss problems or emotions; don't focus on "right" vs. "wrong"; don't focus solely on weight, food, drugs, alcohol, injury, or specific external factors unless there is an emergency; don't try to "fix" the problem yourself; don't engage in communication that is belittling, sarcastic, hostile or patronizing.

The first "**E**" of this plan involves encouraging professional help. In Non-Crisis situations, consider encouraging professional help from:

- Counselors, mental health professionals, medical doctors, social workers, substance abuse counselors, certified peer specialists
- Types of Professional Treatment may include Individual Therapy; Family Therapy; Group Therapy; Medication; Rehab. Programs – Note! Medication is

part of the spectrum of care with medical professional involvement. It is not the role of the MHFAider to diagnose the need for medication.

- If the leader is working with someone who does not want professional support, consider asking, "Who can you talk to that you trust about this?" Never threaten. Remain patient. Remember, "The day you plant the seed is not the day you pick the fruit."

The second "**E**" of this plan involves encouraging self-help and other support strategies. In Non-Crisis situations, consider encouraging self-help.

- People use their own efforts to cope with problems and achieve mental wellness. Their strategies might include relaxation training, exercise, proper nutrition, and sleep.
- You might ask, "What has worked for you before?"
- Not everyone is ready or willing to try self-help – encourage them to come up with possible solutions.

Emergency medical services should be sought if the person has any of the following symptoms:

- Chest pains; Breathing difficulty; serious wound or injury; fainting/unconscious; collapse or too weak to walk; painful muscle spasms; unintentionally throwing up several times a day; blood in BM, urine, or vomit; Irregular or very low heartbeat; cold or clammy skin indicating low body temperature; took overdose of substance or consumed poison.

Like with the myths and facts we addressed with immigrants, educational leaders must use their superpowers of Intentional Noticing to address the following Suicide Myths and Facts:

- Myth: Asking a youth about suicide will only make them angry and increase the risk of suicide.
    - **Fact: Asking someone directly about suicidal**

intent lowers anxiety, opens up communication and lowers the risk.

- Myth: Suicidal kids keep their plans to themselves.
    - **Fact: Most suicidal kids communicate their intent sometime during the week preceding their attempt.**
- Myth: Those who talk about suicide don't do it.
    - **Fact: People who talk about suicide may try, or even complete.**
- Myth: Once a child decides to complete suicide, there is nothing anyone can do to stop them.
    - **Fact: Suicide is the most preventable kind of death, and almost any positive action may save a life.**

If there is a risk of suicide, take immediate action to keep the person safe. Here is a partial listing:

- Do not leave them alone.
- Discuss past supporters and see if they are still available.
- Do not use guilt or threats to prevent suicide.
- Implement the other steps of the ALGEE Action plan.
- Seek additional support of needed, including 911 or 988.
- If an educational leader is called upon to report their assessment views, it is important that they refuse to negate the risk. They should NOT suggest or report that there is "low risk."

There are guidelines to consider when talking to a person who may be suicidal. The following guidelines should be considered:

- Talk in a calm non-accusatory manner.
- Appear confident and empathetic.
- Encourage the person to share their feelings.
- Focus on concern for their well-being.
- Instill hope by asking about long-term plans/goals – let them know that feelings do not last forever.
- If the person is a youth, help speak to their parents/ guardians. Encourage parents/ guardians to seek professional help.

- If the educational leader does not feel that they can keep the person safe, call 911 immediately.

In these situations, the decision to intervene is not easy, even for the most self-assured, confident educational leadership giant. I was impressed by the thoughts of a suicide survivor, Kevin Hynes, who recovered from a suicidal plunge from the Golden Gate Bridge. He created a video to express his feelings about his experiences and the need for people to spring into action, even when it is very likely to be uncomfortable. Here is the video link:

- https://video.link/ https://www.youtube.com/watch?v=WcSUs9iZv-g

Teachers, administration, custodians, lunch personnel, substitutes, nurses, coaches, and coaching staff, even volunteers should be trained regarding suicide awareness and prevention, and the establishment of a conflict resolution process should be required. The training should be required of all students starting in grade 3 (3) and through grade twelve (12) each academic year.

The training that was the source of much of the ideas I suggested above, was sourced from the Mental Health First Aid for Youth (MHFA) program. The program must be taught with fidelity. Check for updated requirements and time commitments involved in MHFA. The program I completed was a three (3) day workshop, and the staff trainings I led ran six to eight (6-8) hours. The "Signs of Suicide" program offers another excellent training option. Here is a video link description: https://www.sprc.org/resources-programs/sos-signs-suicide .

Some school districts have had great success with this program as part of a comprehensive effort. This involves intentional leadership with a formal "Social Emotional Mental Health Coordinator" position, staffed by a lead school psychologist.

USING TESTS, GRADES AND SELF ASSESSMENTS IN EDUCATIONAL LEADERSHIP

HAVE YOU EVER SEEN; "ACHIEVING HIGH TEST SCORES" INCLUDED IN A SCHOOL'S MISSION STATEMENT?

I have often seen schools and districts celebrated as "high performing" and "successful" and others as "failing," "low performing," or worse. The people making and assigning these life-changing labels have very often never visited the schools or even interviewed students and school personnel. Compounding this situation are politicians and other budgetary decision-makers who take these labels and allow them to shape policy.

Test results are consistently an important part of these classifications and judgements, yet I have never seen "...achieving high test scores" appear in any of the school and district mission and goals statements. Educators resist initiatives that are labeled, "teaching to the test." This reflects different *PERSPECTIVES.* The general public sees test results as "objective" evidence of school success or failure. Understanding *Perspectives* on the uses and limits of tests and assessments are essential to educational leadership giant success.

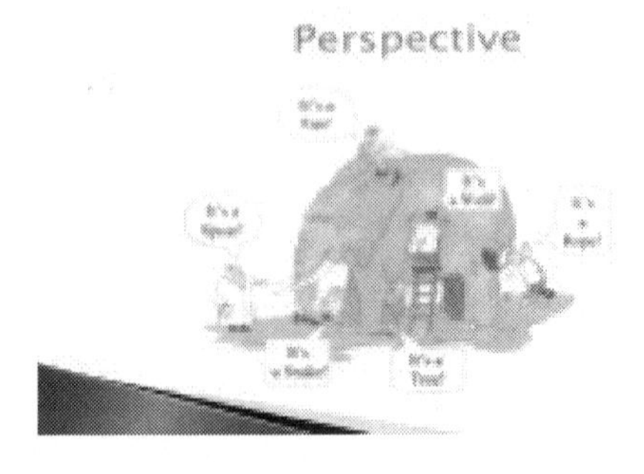

The cartoon with the elephant is a popular display of the inter-relationships between objective data and perspectives. It shows very smart, highly qualified, blindfolded "scientists," making "research-based" informed statements about what they are touching. In all probability they could make forceful arguments to back up their statements. Our perspective, with a great deal more information, leads us to a much different conclusion. We see that they are touching an elephant. How could we convince those "scientists"?

Thanks to Adam Grant, ***(The power of knowing what you don't know) – Think Again***) I now put quotation marks around the word scientist when I use this analogy. In reality, if you are a scientist, by trade, rethinking is fundamental to your profession. You're paid to be constantly aware of the limits of your understanding. You're expected to doubt what you know, be curious about what you don't know, and update your views based on new data.

Mental horsepower doesn't guarantee mental dexterity. No matter how much brain power you have, if you lack the motivation to change your mind, you'll miss many opportunities to think again. There are at least two biases that drive this pattern. One is confirmation bias: seeing what we expect to see. The other is desirability bias: seeing what we want to see.

My favorite bias, like Adam Grant, is the "I'm not biased" bias, in which people believe they're more objective than others. It turns out that smart people are more likely to fall into this trap. The brighter you are, the harder it can be to see your own limitations. Being good at thinking can make you worse at rethinking.

Perhaps if the characters in the cartoon behave like real scientists, they will share their perspectives and ideas with each other and conduct other experiments until they get a better picture of the Elephant. This may be a simple solution, but simple does not mean easy. This is especially true when it comes to perspectives on assessments in general and grading in particular. Toxic grading practices are firmly entrenched in many settings. In some cases, it is a problem of outdated PERSPECTIVES that is causing the difficulty. I have participated in many grading reform workgroups and districtwide initiatives. These efforts are challenging on so very many levels. I am sure you can imagine the political backlash of challenging long held beliefs. Even coming to agreement on the purpose of grading was contentious! There are distinctly different perspectives on the purpose of grading. The first perspective is that grades are meant to discriminate among students and to identify differences in their performance [normative basis]. The second perspective is that grades reflect the degree to which students have learned, accomplished, or achieved what they were taught [criterion basis]. If your purpose is to develop talent, the first thing you do is <u>specify what you want ALL students to learn and be able to do [i.e. learning goals or standards].</u> Once that is settled you do everything possible to ensure that they all learn those things well. If you succeed, there should be little or no variation in measures of student achievement. Grades should reflect students' performance based on specific learning criteria. Considerations of student citizenship and effort, when combined with measures of content knowledge can obscure the validity.

If someone proposed combining measures of height, weight, diet, and exercise into a single number or mark to represent a person's physical condition, we would consider it laughable.

How could the combination of such diverse measures (i.e., scales of inches, pounds, calorie intake per day, and number of minutes of exercise per day) yield anything meaningful?

We need to teach students to be accountable and take responsibility for their actions. Responsibility, punctuality, and respect are important. How do we differentiate between *irresponsible high achievers and highly responsible low achievers?* Multiple Grades! Teachers sometimes give separate grades for product, process, progress criteria, effort, and citizenship.

There are times in the classroom where students give up on challenging, important assignments and are willing to get a poor grade rather than continue to work. In other cases, assigning zeros in a 0-100 averaging grading system can lead to mathematical failure early in the grading period and resulting student disengagement.

This was the case in one of my high schools in my very first administrative assignment. Early in the school year, I caught a student wandering the halls during his science period. When I questioned him, he replied that he had failed the course for the year, and the teacher did not want him in class. I assured him that this was not the case and escorted him back to the room. [**Full disclosure, in reflection, I see where I could have handled aspects of this situation much better**. *As the situation unfolded, I showed my anger in a way that the teacher perceived as disrespectful.*]

When we entered the classroom the teacher said, "What are you doing here? I told you I would probably see you in summer school!" After I confirmed that this was the student's assigned class and got him settled I met with the teacher after class. He showed me his grade book and a series of zero's for missed assignments for the student. He said that even if the student got all "A's" or one hundred's (100's) for the rest of the marking period, he could not pass for the year. This was October!

I asked the teacher what he wanted the student to know and be able to do at this point in the grading period. He was unable to answer this question and reverted to the average grades and their mathematical implications. When I told him that I wasn't questioning his mathematics and sought to develop a plan to help the student succeed in his class, he replied that those efforts were for "Super Star Teachers," and that he was just a "Regular Teacher." My anger must have been clearly visible, because at that point he said he wanted to end the conference and resume with his union building delegate present.

Follow up meetings with the support of other administrators and representatives finally led to resolution. I learned a great deal from this situation, including the danger of the zero in 0-100 grading systems. Comprehensive grading reform is needed to eliminate this and other "Toxic Grading Practices."

Instead of giving a zero for work that is missed, neglected, or turned in late, many teachers assign an "I" or Incomplete grade, and then require students to do additional work to bring their performance up to an acceptable level. They may be required to attend after-school, lunchtime, or even Saturday study sessions.

Successful leaders report that they let parents know about this policy and gained their cooperation with it. This has proven effective for them vs. the total lack of evidence in the research that shows assigning zeros helps teach students better accountability for their work. Similarly, no research supports the idea that low grades prompt students to try harder. More often, low grades lead students to withdraw from learning (Guskey, 2011; Selby & Murphy 1992). As suggested by Douglas Reeves, educational leadership giants should set policies to ensure that grades in all classrooms are:

- ***Accurate*** – The same piece of student work receives the same grade regardless of who the teacher is.
- ***Fair*** – Differences in grades should reflect variations in the quality of work, not differences in gender, ethnicity, or social class.
- ***Timely*** – Students and parents should be told about grades early enough to correct problems.
- ***Understandable*** – Students should get detailed information about how to improve, not just a summative grade or comment (Reeves, 2006).

Perspectives on Grading Practices are often very firmly entrenched. While leadership teams work to reform grading practices, we need to expand views on the ways grades and assessments are used to make important decisions. I have seen a few easy fixes as long as they are carefully communicated to all stakeholders.

Instead of 0-100 some of my schools and numerous teachers in other schools went to a 0,1,2,3,4 system similar to those commonly used in colleges. In this case the numbers convert to 0=F, 1=D, 3=B, 4=A. The mathematics of this system vs. the 0-100 plan can dramatically improve accuracy and mitigate the unreasonable impact of the zero (0).

If current practice requires a 0-100 grade on the report cards you can certainly convert a 0,1,2,3,4 grade as needed. The 0-4 system can include as many decimal points to the right of the number as needed (e.g., a 4.3 can become a "93" on the report card. This requires keeping standards and expectations clear. Contrary to popular misconceptions, computerized grade book systems can be adjusted by educational leaders to reflect levels of mastery. Grading technology is a tool. ***Don't let the tail wag the dog!***

CELEBRATING AND RESPECTING DIVERSE POPULATIONS AT SCHOOL AND AT WORK

What does it mean for educational leaders to create an ethical culture of respect that celebrates diversity? It means embracing ethical standards of leadership behavior with an intentional growth mindset on celebrating the diverse elements in our communities.

Culture is not vague and mysterious...Culture always expresses itself through specific values and observable, measurable behaviors. How do people treat each other in the organization? Morality is generally concerned with how people conduct themselves and is based on a personal value system heavily influenced by one's culture.

Think about how you would describe the concept of "ethics." What would you want your audience to understand? The umbrella concept is trust that the right things are done, and people are treated right. It is a real source of pride when a profession has its own code of ethics. I found some commonalities in reviewing the published ethical standards of various education-related professions that include the following. Ethical standards are designed to (a) protect public consumers and improve delivery of services to diverse groups of clients, (b) promote accountability and stability of the organization by reinforcing established standards, (c) educate members about what is considered desired ethical conduct, (d) provide a framework in the ethical decision-making process when ethical dilemmas arise, and (e) protect professionals delivering services from licensure board complaints and malpractice suits from consumers.

Please note that protection and safety is a prominent theme. In my work with outstanding law enforcement and security leaders, I found that RELATIONSHIPS are essential factors in safety. Confidentiality is required to develop healthy relationships. For school leaders, it is important to clearly communicate the limits of confidentiality, especially in our work with students.

To avoid causing relationship damage, they must understand that some areas may not be kept confidential. I use the acronym CASH to describe those areas: Child Abuse, Sexual abuse, Suicide, Homicide (CASH). Anything that involves imminent danger carries a duty to report. The Signs of Suicide (SOS) program addresses this in a comprehensive manner.

Ethics creates an umbrella culture that helps our work with multicultural groups. Culture is NOT a race, nationality, or birthplace! Culture is the set of shared attitudes, values, goals, and practices. It is learned behavior. We must be aware of Cultural differences in learning-related activities and opportunities. This requires a healthy degree of intentional self-understanding. Indeed, leadership giant competence begins with self-understanding regarding diversity. What values are dear? How would leaders proceed with those whose value structure was significantly different?

By 2050 almost fifty percent of the population in the United States will be minorities. Leaders must learn about different cultures by embracing these differences. In individualistic cultures such as those in Europe and North America, a great amount of value is placed on individual accomplishment. Individuals strive for self-actualization.

In collectivist cultures such as those in Africa, Asia, and Latin America, the individual's major function is focused on the welfare of the group for their collective survival. Mutual respect is also a large part of the culture.

European immigrants experienced exclusion and poverty during the first two waves of immigration in the 19th and 20th centuries. Eventually, these immigrants transformed this country with significant changes that included enlightenment and acceptance of diversity. People of color, however, continue to struggle for acceptance.

Gender stereotyping is a significant obstacle that needs to be removed to promote shared life and work roles. A person's gender-related behaviors can be modified or sustained by contemporary experiences, and reflection on these experiences.

DID YOU REALLY THINK THAT WAS AN APPROPRIATE COMPLIMENT?

One of my favorite assignments in the business world, prior to my career in education, involved serving as an interim personnel manager for a textile manufacturing firm. In addition to playing a role in hiring the right people, I was responsible for investigating claims of sexual harassment.

One case stands out. I had a female employee storm into my office visibly upset. She said, "You have to do something about that pig, Roger!... If you don't I will!!" She calmed down and related the details of the incident involving Roger. When I called him into my office, Roger appeared a little surly. He said, "I know why I'm here. All I said was that she looked good, and she went off on me like I did something awful to her!" "I think she may have psychological problems." I asked him to describe the incident in detail.

He said that he noticed the dress that she was wearing and said she looked good. He insisted that this was the complete description. I proceeded to relate the other details that I knew from the complaining employee's report, verified in part by plant wide area video recordings. What he really said was that her dress really brought out her figure, and he made gestures with both of his hands. Seeing the video recording added impact! He volunteered that he "kids around all the time with her and other co-workers." He was held accountable for his behavior. The incident and resulting interventions had a lasting impact on company culture.

Appropriate interactions between women and men in schools and workplaces must be taught. Sexual harassment is the single most widespread occupational hazard women face in the workforce. It is a form of bullying – Appropriate interactions between women and men in the workplace and among female and male students must be taught. Humor can be helpful in relationships. Some things cannot and should not be the topic of jokes – lines are crossed in unacceptable ways. The leader must encourage people to object to behaviors they find objectionable! Clearly, There is nothing easy about this!

Teaching healthy interpersonal behaviors impacts school and business culture. Giving positive feedback and praise is an essential leadership skill. Genuine compliments build relationships, improve communication, motivate people, and boost self-esteem and self-confidence. Praise and genuine, appropriate compliments have power to build up the receiver and the giver.

In professional settings, leader compliments involving someone's physical appearance are ill advised, and sometimes viewed as offensive. There are great ways to compliment others without commenting on physical appearance. Below are some of my favorites, and the website source. The links within the article are also important to our work.

https://iheartintelligence.com/compliments-you-can-give/

People often give compliments based on the appearance of others, since we find it easy to judge someone based on appearance.
Here are a few compliments you can rely on to help build others up without commenting on their bodies.

For number six (6) on the original list, I substituted the word "fortunate" for "lucky."

1. **I'm impressed by how resilient you are.**
   Have you ever known someone who was just so strong they could withstand a tornado of difficulty? Resilient people are awesome, and this is a great compliment to give someone who is especially resilient.

2. **You're such a good listener.**
   There are a lot of people in the world who don't actually listen, instead waiting for their turn to speak. Finding a good listener can be like finding a needle in a haystack! If you know someone who you think is a good listener, tell them so!

3. **I like how authentic you are.**
   Authentic people are on a whole different level! Authenticity means not hiding the person they are on the inside. To be authentic requires a great deal of confidence and security. If you know an authentic person, tell them how much you admire that about them.

4. **I admire how hard you work.**
   If you've ever worked with someone who cuts corners and doesn't work all that hard, it really makes people who do work hard stand out. If you've got a co-worker who works especially hard, forget their body – tell them how much you admire their work ethic!

5. You are dependable.

Sometimes it can seem like everyone depends on you, but you can't really depend on anyone but yourself. Still, once in a while, you meet someone who you can lean on whenever you need to and vice versa. Tell them you appreciate how dependable they are!

6. I'm fortunate **(lucky) to know you.**

This might be my favorite compliment on this list. There are a lot of people in this world. We are truly fortunate (lucky) to have the people we do in our lives. Tell them so! I feel so good giving out this compliment and receiving it too.

7. Your laugh is contagious.

Have you ever known someone whose laugh can just make a room erupt? They're one of my favorite kinds of people. Telling them how contagious their laugh is will help them laugh more easily.

8. I am amazed by your progress.

If you know someone working hard towards a goal, tell them how much you admire the progress they've made. It'll help keep them going!

9. You're a strong person.

Even the strongest people in the world feel weak from time to time. It helps to be reminded by others that you are, in fact, an incredibly strong person.

10. Everyone loves you.

The world can be filled with love, or it can be filled with hate. It really is our choice. For me, I choose love over hate. And I like to remind the amazing people in my life that they are loved. It's a kind thing to do.

GENDER DIVERSITY AND THE EDUCATIONAL LEADER

Educational leaders need to take an active role in challenging outdated stereotypes in an effort to expand perceptions of appropriate life and career pathways. This is especially important in considering gender diversity.

Sexual orientation should be viewed as only one factor to consider in career and life pathways exploration and decisions. Individuals need to know that they are not alone, abnormal, or unwell. Times and attitudes have changed, and the language used to discuss sexual orientation and gender identity has also changed. A number of former students and colleagues expanded my knowledge of terminology related to sexual orientation. **Christina Ingemi**, in particular, was extremely influential. What follows is a brief glossary of eighteen (18) or so, terms that may be useful, starting with the common LGBTQ2S+ acronym:

1. **L – Lesbian**: a female-identified person who is physically and emotionally attracted to other females.
2. **G – Gay**: a male-identified person who is physically and emotionally attracted to other males. Gay is also used as a broad term to describe people attracted to someone of the same gender.
3. **B – Bisexual/Bi**: a person who is physically and emotionally attracted to people of more than one gender and who identifies as bisexual (bi).
4. **T – Transgender/Trans**: transgender (trans) is a term used by people who identify with a gender that is different from the gender they were assigned at birth. People whose gender identity falls outside of the gender binary (the idea that there are only two genders — male and female) may also call themselves trans. Since trans is a word used to describe identity, a person has to identify with the term (believe it's the best way to describe themselves) for it to

be applicable. No one else can decide a person is or isn't trans. Other terms to describe gender identity that may be preferred by some people include genderqueer, gender fluid and androgynous. **DO NOT USE TRANSVESTITE, THIS IS A DEROGATORY TERM. IMPORTANT TO NOTE THAT TRANS FOLK CAN IDENTIFY WITH OR WITHOUT RECONSTRUCTIVE SURGERY OR HORMONE TREATMENTS.** *Trans is not a sexual orientation — it's a gender identity. "T" (for transgender/trans) is grouped with the sexual orientations in LGBTQ2S+ for many reasons, including shared civil and human rights activism and similar experiences of discrimination.*

5. **Q – Queer**: queer is a broad term that includes all sexual orientations and gender identities within the LGBTQIA2S+ community, including those who don't identify with any other identity in LGBTQIA2S+. The term queer can be both positive and negative. Historically, queer was used as an insult, but it has been reclaimed by the LGBTQ2S+ community to self-identify in a positive way.
6. **Q – Questioning**: some people may feel unsure about their sexual orientation and/or gender identity. They may describe themselves as questioning. They may be questioning until they identify with a particular identity or continue to be questioning throughout their lives.
7. **Intersex**: intersex describes when a person is born with both male and female sex organs or other sexual characteristics. Some intersex individuals are assigned a gender at birth that they're raised as, which may or may not fit with how they view their gender identity.
8. **A - Asexual (ace):** a person who doesn't experience physical attraction to other people but may still have emotional attraction to others.
9. **Agender**: a person who doesn't identify with any gender or identifies as being genderless. Their gender identity may live outside of the gender binary. Agender people may or may not identify as transgender (trans).

10. **Two-Spirit (2 Spirit or 2S)**: a person with both a feminine and a masculine spirit living in the same body. It's an important term within some Indigenous cultures and some Indigenous people use it to describe their sexual orientation, gender identity and/or spiritual identity. This differs from nation to nation. Here is a helpful resource. ***THIS IDENTITY IS NOT FOR NON-INDIGENOUS FOLKS**
11. **Sexual orientations**: Your students are going to be in relationships that you may be unfamiliar with. It's okay to ask questions, and it's also your responsibility to have some understanding of the world of queer relationships. We live in a heteronormative world - do your part by at the very least understanding people operate outside of this reality. Assuming of boyfriend/ girlfriend is no longer acceptable in 2021.
12. **Pansexual (pan)**: a person who experiences sexual, romantic, physical, emotional and/or spiritual attraction to members of all gender identities/gender expressions.
13. **Demisexual**: People who identify as demisexual only feel sexual attraction to another person if they form a strong emotional bond or connection with them first.
14. **Sapiosexuality**: a person who identifies as Sapio has a limited number of people to whom they may be attracted. a person who identifies as sapiosexual is attracted to intelligence or the mind of the other person. Here, the emotional bond is not the crucial factor.
15. **Gender identities:** Using terms like boys and girls is no longer universally acceptable. Work to shift your vocabulary into something more inclusive. (He/she is very easily shifted to they/them) or boys and girls very easily be changed to folks. **DO THE WORK TO CHANGE THIS. DON'T STAY COMFORTABLE IN THE BINARY. DOING THIS IMPACTS THE SAFETY OF YOUR STUDENTS. This is difficult for me, and I frequently find myself using the boys and girls terminolo-**

gy. You might even see older school buildings with the words "Boys" and "Girls" carved right into the concrete to designate the separate playground areas that were used when the buildings were constructed.

A. **Gender fluid**: a person whose gender identity and gender expression are not static and can shift with time and/or circumstance.
B. **Genderqueer**: a person who identifies as neither, both or a mix of male and female. Individuals who identify as genderqueer may or may not also identify as trans.
C. **Non-binary**: a person who doesn't accept a society that only acknowledges the gender binary of male and female and defines their gender outside of those norms. People who are non-binary may identify as having no gender, feel in between genders or have a gender that is not always the same. Individuals who identify as non-binary may or may not also identify as trans.

16. **Aromantic (aro)**: aromantic is a romantic orientation (who a person is emotionally attracted to). Aromantic describes a person who doesn't experience emotional attraction (feelings like love, connection, etc.) to others.
17. **Polyamory**: a relationship style in which individuals have intimate relationships with more than one person at once. This happens with the full knowledge and consent of all partners involved.
18. **Romantic orientation**: romantic orientation refers to how people are emotionally attracted to others (feelings like love, connection, etc.). A person's romantic orientation may be the same as, or different than, their sexual orientation.

It is important to note that sexual and gender identity is multifaceted. Not every person fits into a box. When leaders hear intentional insensitive slurs, they must treat the comment like any other slur; in fact, holding people accountable for racist comments while evading homophobic remarks would indirectly legitimize anti-LGBTQIA+ attacks.

Leaders must take an active role in challenging stereotypes. Sexual orientation should be viewed as only one factor to consider.

PEOPLE WITH DISABILITIES

Any comprehensive discussion on the celebration of diversity includes embracing people with disABILITIES. Leaders must recognize that people with disABILITIES are an extremely diverse group that share some common elements of thinking and behaving and yet have unique needs.

A few facts may help gain perspective. There are over fifty-six million Americans, and six hundred fifty million individuals globally with disABILITIES. It is important that leaders concentrate on what people can do rather than what they can't. A recent quote from the talented interpreter who signs for people who cannot hear is revealing. He was asked if he could gain his hearing, would he do it? His answer was, No. He said people who are deaf are not broken, and in need of fixing.

Dr. Kate McCarthy-Barnett has worked for the US Department of Homeland Security Federal Emergency Management Agency, as one of the first Regional Disability Integration Specialists across the country. For ten years she also wrote a column for the Providence Journal Newspaper called "disABILITY" where she explored and addressed challenges encountered by those with disABILITIES, and highlighted people who overcame adversity to lead productive lives. She visited my graduate class at Providence College and shared the following Guide for communicating with people with disABILITIES. She advises that:

- ***When you talk with a person, who has a disABILITY, speak directly to them rather than through a person who is with them.***
- ***When you are introduced to a person with a disABILITY, it is OK to shake hands with the left hand***

if the person has limited right hand use or an artificial limb.

- *When meeting a person who is blind, always identify yourself and others who may be with you. When there are many people in a group, identify the person to whom you are speaking. Many people who are blind are very sensitive to loud noises and may need extra consideration in group conversations.*
- *If you want to help a person with a disABILITY, ask them first, and then listen to or ask for instructions on how to help.*
- *Give the person respect. Just as you would not pat an adult without a disABILITY on the head or lean on them as you speak, you should not lean on a person's wheelchair or pat them on the head like a pet.*
- *Listen carefully with your eyes and your ears when you are talking with a person who has difficulty speaking. Be patient and wait for the person to finish, rather than correcting or trying to speak for the person. Never pretend to understand if you are having difficulty doing so. Instead, repeat what you have understood and allow the person to respond.*
- *To get the attention of a person who is deaf tap the person on the shoulder or wave your hand. Look directly at the person and speak clearly, slowly and use a lot of gestures. Not all people who are deaf can read lips.*
- *Relax. Don't be embarrassed or afraid of a person just because they may have a disABILITY.*
- *Ask questions when you are unsure what to do.*

Leaders must understand that people with disABILITIES are an extremely diverse population. Great strides have been made in understanding neurodiversity.

Neurodiversity involves natural variances in the brain which result in different ways of learning, thinking, and socializing.

This is a vast, and underused resource for amazing talent. This is especially true for people with Autism Spectrum "Disorder" (ASD). I added the quotation marks around the word "disorder," because it sometimes limits perspectives on the strengths and advantages involved.

According to the Centers for Disease Control (CDC) AutismSpeaks.org, ASD is primarily characterized by communication difficulties, social/interpersonal barriers, repetitive and restrictive behaviors and interests. One in sixty-eight children in the United States have ASD. Ten to fourteen percent of U.S. college students have ASD. Forty percent have an average or higher IQ, and many have exceptional visual, academic, and musical abilities. Repetitive behaviors and routines are often used to cope with academic and social anxieties. It is amazing that fewer than one in six autistic adults are employed full time in spite of some outstanding Strengths and Advantages. Very often people with ASD have the following strengths:

- They can hyper-focus on one area of study, leading to subject mastery,
- They are rarely distracted by or mixed-up in social or office politics.
- In college settings they are almost twice as likely to major in a STEM-related field
- They can often be relied upon to follow-through and follow-up.

Other strength-based approaches that I like to call "Coolabilities," are characteristics of people with the following differences:

Those with Autism often:

- Have deep passions and interests and may be particularly skilled in one area.
- Are very honest and loyal.
- Are very detail oriented.
- Can engage in repetitive tasks.

- Are punctual and rarely miss work.
- Are strong visual thinking.
- Are logical.
- Are great at pattern recognition.

Those with language-based dyslexia often:

- Have great spatial reasoning and global visual processing skills.
- See the "bigger picture."
- Have great pattern recognition.
- Are highly creative.
- Are strong visual thinkers.
- Have strong problem-solving ability.

Those with ADHD/ADD often:

- Are creative and highly attentive.
- Have the ability to hyperfocus on an area of interest and can have a high level of productivity.
- Are perceptive and notice changes.
- They have strong problem-solving skills.

When social relationships are formed, they can become some of the most dependable friends that one could want. I have often found that organizations that do good, also do well!

Regarding embracing diversity, the research bears this out. Organizations with differently abled employees outperform their competitors, averaging 28% higher revenue plus higher stakeholder returns (Hyland & Connolly, 2018). In spite of this, individuals with intellectual and developmental differences have an 85% unemployment rate (Moss, 2019). This is an area where educational leadership giants can enrich their organizations and their lives through an intentional effort to recruit and retain differently abled individuals.

BULLYING AND MEAN BEHAVIOR – (SCHOOL SETTINGS)

"IF IT'S MEAN...INTERVENE!"

People with disABILITIES and other members of diverse populations are disproportionately bullied and subjected to mean behaviors. Bullying involves a perceived power imbalance that is not always apparent in other types of mean behaviors. Rather than getting hung up on definitions, I stick with the mantra for leaders, "If it's MEAN…INTERVENE!" This intervention can take many forms.

Bullying and mean behavior has reached epidemic proportions in American schools and communities.

- Sixty-six percent of youth are teased at least once a month, and nearly one-third of youth are targeted for bullying at least once a month.
- Six out of 10 American teens witness bullying and mean behavior at least once a day.
- Victims of bullying and mean behaviors are more likely to suffer physical problems such as common colds and coughs, sore throats, poor appetite.
- Those who are bullied are five times more likely to be depressed and far more likely to be suicidal. Suicide is the number two cause of death among youth.

Here are some tips to help respond more effectively on the spot and make the best use of the "teachable moment" with all students at school. In some cases, I have added the word "mean" along with "bullying." When adults see or hear bullying or mean behaviors they should: ***Immediately stop the bullying:*** Stand between the child or children who bullied and those who were bullied, preferably blocking eye contact between them. They should not send any students away – especially bystanders. They should avoid immediately asking about or discussing the reason for the bullying or try to sort out the facts.

Reference should be made to the school rules against the mean behavior in a matter-of-fact tone of voice, stating the behaviors that were observed. (e.g., "Calling someone names is mean behavior and is against our school rules.") The target of the bullying behavior must be supported in a way that allows them to regain self-control, to "save face," and to feel supported and safe from retaliation.

Follow up is essential. This should be done later, in private if they are upset. They should not be asked what happened at the time of the incident. It can be very uncomfortable to be questioned in front of other students. The child should be seen later, in private if they are upset. Other appropriate staff should be notified about the incident so that they may provide additional support and protection. Supervision should be increased to assure that the bullying is not repeated and does not escalate.

Bystanders should not be put on the spot to explain publicly what they observed. In a calm, matter of fact, supportive tone of voice, they should be told that their inaction was noticed or that the way they tried to help was appreciated. They should be encouraged to take a more active or pro social role next time. All consequences should be logical and connected to the offense. Students who bully should know that they, and their friends will be watched closely to be sure there is no retaliation. Unlike some other kinds of conflict, bullying involves a power imbalance, which means the strategy of having the students meet and "work things out," is not advised. This can re-traumatize the target student and it does not generally improve relationships between the parties.

Instead, the aggressor should be encouraged to make amends in a way (after follow-up with an adult) that would be meaningful for the child who was bullied. Staff members who provide follow-up are likely to need specialized skills or training as well as enough time to investigate problems, to administer appropriate discipline, or to provide therapeutic intervention. Different types of situations and levels of severity of bullying incidents require follow-up intervention from adults and designates.

Targets of bullying and mean behaviors need to process the circumstance of the bullying, vent their feelings about it, and get support. Some may need assistance reading or interpreting social signals, practicing assertive behavior, building self-esteem, or identifying friends and classmates who can give them support. They need a "go-to trusted adult!"

Students who bully may need help recognizing their behavior, taking responsibility for their behavior, developing empathy and perspective-taking abilities, and finding ways to make amends. They may also need help to learn how to use power in socially appropriate ways (e.g., focusing their energy on causes they care about).

When there are suspicions of bullying, more information should be gathered by talking privately with bystanders. Observation and supervision should be intensified, and incentives or positive consequences offered to active, helpful, bystanders to increase involvement by students. To be successful, bystanders need opportunities to discuss and practice responses outside of the heat of the moment. The more options they have, the more successful they will be.

Leaders must intervene to address bullying and mean behaviors in a comprehensive manner. That involves recognizing that adults see only about 20% of the bullying and mean behaviors.

This also relates to bullying in the workplace. Other students and co-workers see the vast majority, 80% of the bullying and mean behaviors. In addition to immediately intervening to stop the bullying, educational leadership giants must empower bystanders to become *upstanders.* Providing students with a trusted, go-to adult is a major protective factor against bullying trauma.

THE IMPORTANCE OF THE EDUCATIONAL LEADER AS THE "GO-TO PERSON!"

Parents of children who are involved in incidents of bullying and mean behaviors should be notified. There may also be others that require reports. In my schools, as principal, I wanted to be notified before parents were contacted so that I could support the entire process, and everyone involved!

Warning: [LANGUAGE] I am intentional about avoiding course, vulgar, or obscene language, especially in professional situations. I have been told that this may be due to my "Baby-Boomer" status. My reply is…I have seen situations take unexpected negative turns when leaders used vulgar language. Even a promising political campaign and career came crashing down because of an unfortunate crude remark. That said, the following leadership lesson includes vulgar, rude, and swearing language that is essential to understanding the situation. As with all of the lesson stories, the names have been changed.

As a principal, I advised my teachers to come to me right away if they should ever "lose it" and say or do something inappropriate involving a student, parent, or colleague. One of my high school teachers came into my office in tears and sobbed that he had lost it in class, and in a fit of anger, threw an Expo Marker over the head of a student.

He went on to relate the details of the incident and offered to resign. I thanked him for coming to me in a timely manner. I had a positive relationship from past interactions with the student and parent involved. I called the parent right away. The conversation went like this:

ALBA "Hi Regina, it's Doc Alba from school, your daughter Samantha is fine, no one was harmed in any way, but I want to tell you about a situation that just happened in class. Samantha was in Mr. Conte's class, and she stood up and shouted, "You're a fuckin faggot!" She said this more than once and then laughing sat back down. The teacher lost it and threw a marker that hit the white board over her head. We both know that's not right Regina and you also know I will be holding him accountable, and that behavior will never, ever be repeated! Samantha then stood up and said, 'My mother is going to come to school and kick your ass!' I wanted you to know about this situation right away. She is likely to come home and have a version of the situation that leaves out a few things."

PARENT (REGINA) "Thanks Dr. A. I know my daughter, that little Bitch has quite a nasty mouth! I will take care of her when she gets home. You take care of that teacher!"

Without the advanced phone call, this situation would have likely escalated in dramatic ways. In later conversations with Regina, she remarked how Samantha rushed home and excitedly reported that a teacher threw a marker at her for no reason at all! Regina replied, I talked to Dr. Alba and know all about it, so don't lie and leave stuff out! It is all being taken care of. Now let's talk about that mouth of yours!

8 LEADERS KEEPING PEOPLE SAFE

After a tragic, violent attack on one of their employees, I was approached by a large insurance company (the one that partnered with my school) to facilitate personal safety workshops. I worked with numerous experts in the field to develop a comprehensive, solution-focused approach to this highest priority challenge. Special thanks to **Police Chief Anthony Pesare** for his advice and input.

Educational leadership giants must be intentional about their own personal safety as they address these issues within their communities. This requires them to gain the following specific competencies and share them, with fidelity, in a comprehensive manner. They must:

- Learn the difference between personal safety and self-defense.
- Recognize risk factors to reduce threats.
- Learn to recognize and avoid potentially dangerous situations.
- Learn to control dangerous situations by controlling their own attitude and behavior.
- Learn to respond to aggression with controlled measures.
  - Learn what to do when confronted with aggression.

- Learn techniques to protect themselves.
- Learn how to turn by-standers into up-standers in bullying and mean behavior situations.

SELF-DEFENSE AND PERSONAL SAFETY

Marc MacYoung suggests that there is a big difference between self-defense and personal safety. Self-defense is predicated on the fact that you are in a very bad place to begin with. Things have already gone terribly wrong. As such, self-defense is making sure the situation doesn't get any worse -- it is damage control, pure and simple. However, no damage control is EVER as good as preventing the problem in the first place. That's personal safety...

In recognizing risk factors people can reduce threats. In assessing potential danger consider "Ability," "Opportunity," and "Intent."

PAYING ATTENTION is an essential part of this approach. In school or office settings, the importance of the way each visitor is treated cannot be overstated. Leaders cannot allow themselves to be separated from the first impressions visitors experience. **Amy Cuddy**, a psychologist at the Harvard Business School, has been studying first impressions for more than a decade. She and her colleagues found that we make snap judgments about other people that answer two primary questions: 1. Can I trust this person? 2. Can I respect this person's capabilities?

According to Cuddy's research, 80% to 90% of a first impression is based on these two traits. Subconsciously, you and the people you meet are asking yourselves, "Can I trust that this person has good intentions toward me?" and "Is this person capable?" We often assume that competence is the most important factor, and people tend to play this up when they meet someone; however, Cuddy's research shows that trust is the most important factor. In order for your competence to matter, people must trust you first. If there's no trust, people actually perceive competence as a negative. As Cuddy said, "A warm, trustworthy person who is also strong elicits admiration, but only after you've achieved trust does your strength become a gift rather than a threat."

Since these impressions extend to the whole school, office, or organization, leaders must pay particular attention to the personnel making these first impressions on visitors. Visitors should be greeted as soon as they are noticed! The greeter should introduce themselves, get the person's name and purpose for their visit. Greeters body language should show that they are interested.

While this can often start things off right, greeters must be prepared to deal with difficult visitors. This involves learning to recognize and avoid potentially dangerous situations, learning fundamental approaches to personal safety, controlling their own attitude and behavior, learning
to respond to aggression with controlled measures, learning what to do when confronted with aggression, and learning self-protection techniques.
Personnel must be trained to carefully consider the difficult visitor's Ability, Opportunity, and Intent for danger. When confronted by agitated aggressive individuals they must respond with controlled measures. They shouldn't touch the individual unless they are prepared for a physical altercation. They should always give the person a way out. If all else fails,

they should leave the area and get help. They are not obligated or compelled to resolve the problem at the point of aggression.

There are other fundamental approaches to personal safety that should be addressed. Precautions to decrease opportunities for crimes against you and those you lead include the following. Don't be an easy target. This includes walking carelessly in public with your head buried in your phone. Trust your intuition about potentially dangerous settings and suspected criminals. Stay alert and aware as you plan your travel to include safe havens, lighting, and phone access. Traveling in groups is 70% safer than alone. That said, stopping for strangers can be dangerous, as can alcohol and other intoxicants.

When you are on public transportation, entertainment venues, or shops, be aware of your neighbors as well as the proximity of exits. Criminals have been known to target shoppers carrying many packages, especially those from expensive stores. When walking or jogging it is best to stay alert to surroundings, carry ID, and let someone know your plans. The newer cars have many improved safety features. It is still a good idea to check your area and park safely. Glance into your backseat before you get in your vehicle.

The following approaches are suggested to keep your vehicle safer:

1. **Always Take Your Keys. Never leave them in the car. Nearly 20% of all vehicles stolen had the keys in them.**
2. **Always Lock Your Car. Approximately 50% of all vehicles stolen were left unlocked.**
3. **Park in Well-lighted Areas. Over half of all vehicle thefts occur at night.**
4. **Park in Attended Lots. Auto thieves do not like witnesses and prefer unattended parking lots.**
5. **If you park in an attended lot, leave only the ignition/door key. If your trunk and glove box use the same key**

as the door, have one of them changed. Don't give the attendant easy access to your glove box and trunk.

6. **Never leave your car running, even if you will only be gone for a minute. Vehicles are commonly stolen at convenience stores, gas stations, ATM's, etc. Many vehicles are also stolen on cold mornings when the owner leaves the vehicle running to warm up. Leaving your key in an unattended motor vehicle is a crime in some states.**
7. **Don't Leave Valuables in Plain View. Don't make your car a more desirable target and attract thieves by leaving valuables in plain sight.**
8. **Alarms. Loud warnings sound when doors/hood/trunk are opened. Optional sensors include glass breakage, motion, tampering and towing. Panic buttons, back-up batteries, flashing parking lights or headlights, and automatic engine disable features are also recommended.**
9. **Vehicle Tracking. Transmitters hidden in cars enable police to track cars and enable police and citizens to identify stolen cars.**

FACE TO FACE DANGEROUS SITUATIONS

Respond to aggression with controlled measures when confronted by an agitated aggressive individual. Maintain a calm, composed appearance. It translates to others as a positive sign. Avoid any physical contact if at all possible. Never touch the individual unless you are prepared for a physical altercation. Always give the person a way out. If all else fails, leave the area, and get help. Do not feel obligated or compelled to resolve the problem at the point of aggression. A twenty-dollar bill ($20) can be an excellent tool in a robbery situation. Readily handing over a $20 bill can often de-escalate a mugging situation and send the criminal away.

Responding with controlled measures to a sexual assault is a serious decision – submit or resist – life or death. Talk in a firm but polite manner. Say "NO!" in human terms. Consider the following:

- Can I get away? What are my options?
- Submission doesn't guarantee that there will be no further injury.
- Know what you are getting into BEFORE YOU PHYSICALLY RESIST. Are you mentally prepared to fight forcefully and with extreme violence? CAN you "gouge his eyes," "knee his groin," "jab his Adam's apple," bite, kick and continue to fight when you have been hurt?
- WILL you? Even with years of training it takes a strong will and great determination to put self-defense training into practice.
- If you are sexually assaulted, get to safety, call police, preserve physical evidence, hospital exam, write facts (details), victim support groups.

Here are some facts to consider regarding family violence:

- Majority of Family Violence is Male to Female
- Men also use the threat of violence to control their female partners.
- 65 percent occurred among people who were intimate.
- 41 percent of women homicide victims were killed by their husbands.
- Four percent of the male victims were killed by wives or girlfriends.

When leaders have a better understanding of the causes of aggression, they are better able to keep themselves and others safer. Consider the following basic facts most often cited:

1. Violent behavior is intended to do harm. It can be emotional, to express anger, or instrumental, to attain a goal.
2. It is never acceptable to use violent or harmful behavior to express anger.
3. No matter what has influenced a person to be violent, it is their responsibility to choose to learn nonviolent and helpful ways to express anger.

4. Feelings aren't good or bad, or right or wrong; they just are.
5. Putting thinking between your feelings and your behavior enables you to choose helpful ways to express feelings.
6. Five ways to express anger are stuffing, withdrawing, blaming, exploding, and solution-focused problem solving.
7. Parents usually love their children, even when the parents are choosing to use violent or harmful ways to express their anger.
8. Children usually love their parents, although they may feel hate for the parents if the parents are using violent ways to express their anger.
9. When people are angry about a problem they can't change they should consider:
    1) Accepting what they can't change at the present time
    2) Expressing their anger so they can let it go at the present time
    3) Doing something good for themselves
10. When people are angry about a problem they can change, they should use their anger to give them the power to make changes in themselves by learning to use solution-focused problem-solving skills.
11. The anger management steps (see below) help people put thinking between the feeling of anger and the behavior of anger.
    1. Suggested anger management steps include:
        1) Recognize that you are angry.
        2) Accept your anger
        3) Practice relaxation
        4) Decide if it is a problem you can't change or a problem you can change
        5) Think about helpful and harmful ways to express the anger
        6) Evaluate the consequences and choose a best way
        7) Problem-solve or express your anger in a helpful way.

12. No matter what you believe about the causes, family violence will end only if each person decides never to use violence in his or her own life.
13. To set limits against the use of force in a relationship, it may be helpful to speak in a calm, rational way, firmly, and with conviction and determination.
14. When supporting youth regarding their parents expressing anger help them see that:
    1) Children don't CAUSE their parents to use violence
    2) Children most often can't CONTROL how their parents express anger
    3) Children need support in efforts to CHANGE their parents' use of violence to express anger.
15. The Four steps people can take if they live in a violent family are:
    1) Find a safe place for themselves
    2) Get competent help
    3) Learn to put thinking between their feelings and their behaviors
    4) Choose to learn nonviolent ways to express their own feelings and learn to use problem-solving skills in anger situations.
16. People can't fix other people's problems.
17. People can take good care of themselves.
18. People need to take good care of their bodies, their minds, their feelings, and their choices.

While educational leaders must be concerned and aware of personal safety factors and best protective practices, the decision to actually use the ideas presented is very personal. Each individual carries the major responsibility for their own personal safety.

EDUCATIONAL LEADERS IN ELEMENTARY AND SECONDARY SCHOOL SETTINGS

Archbishop Desmond Tutu said, "There comes a point where we need to stop just pulling people out of the river. We need to go upstream and find out why they're falling in." Going "upstream" for educational leadership giants involves school-based, developmentally appropriate, comprehensive efforts. We start with elementary school leadership.

Student academic success for all, is the primary goal followed by vocational and personal growth goals. In early childhood (2-5 yrs.) Most children have limits in their logical or abstract thinking. This gradually progresses in upper elementary school, where they start to apply logic to thinking and can understand simple concepts. Concrete experiences and consistent generalizations help them see that objects or people fit into more than one category (e.g., police officer is also a little league coach).

WHAT DO YOU WANT TO BE WHEN YOU GROW UP?

"What do you want to be when you grow up?" is a very common, but misguided question that adults ask children. Adam Grant and other psychologists suggest that asking children what they want to be when they grow up can lead to identity foreclosure—when we settle prematurely on a sense of self without enough due diligence and close our minds to alternative selves. In career choices, identity foreclosure often begins when adults ask kids: What do you want to be when you grow up? Pondering that question can foster a fixed mindset about work and self. Grant goes on to say, "I think it's one of the most useless questions an adult can ask a child,"

Michelle Obama in her book, "Becoming" writes ***"What do you want to be when you grow up?*** As if growing up is finite. As if at some point you become something and that's the end." Instead of trying to narrow their options, help them broaden their possibilities. They don't have to be one thing—they can do many things.

Do ask older children,

- What kind of person do you want to be?
- What are all the different things you like to do?
- What problems would you like to solve?
- Do you know some people who are very happy at their jobs? What do they do?

I have used that last questions with students at all age levels to help them focus their interests.

Observational learning, or modeling is a critical factor in child development. Children learn not only from direct, intentional interactions with adults, but also from their observations. Albert Bandura conducted hundreds of studies on this model. One of them really stands out above the others – the bobo doll studies.

Bobo Doll

He made of film of one of his graduate students, a young woman, essentially beating up a bobo doll. In case you don't know, a bobo doll is an inflatable, egg-shaped balloon creature with a weight in the bottom that makes it bob back up when you knock him down. The woman punched the clown, shouting "sockeroo!" She kicked it, sat on it, hit it with a little hammer, and so on, shouting various aggressive phrases.

Bandura showed his film to groups of kindergartners who, as you might predict, liked it a lot. They then were let out to play. Observing the playroom, of course, were several researchers with pens and clipboards in hand. You might predict what the observers recorded: A lot of little kids beating the daylights out of the bobo doll. They punched it and shouted "sockeroo," kicked it, sat on it, hit it with the little hammers, and so on.

In other words, they imitated the young lady in the film, and quite precisely at that. This might seem like a real nothing of an experiment at first but consider: These children changed their behavior without first being rewarded for approximations to that behavior! And while that may not seem extraordinary to the average parent, teacher, or casual observer of children, it didn't fit so well with standard behavioristic learning theory. Bandura called the phenomenon observational learning or modeling, and his theory is usually called social learning theory.

These links show the actual experiment first and then an analysis.

video.link/https://www.youtube.com/watch?v=NjTxQy_U3ac
/video.link/https://www.youtube.com/watch?v=b-ggEEo16jc

The findings support Bandura's Social Learning Behaviorist Theory. That is, children learn social behavior such as aggression through the process of observation learning - through watching the behavior of another person. Central to Social Learning Theory is the identification of which types of models are more likely to be imitated. Leaders must carefully consider the implications of this. The impact on children is so important that collaboration is essential to monitor and guide the full range of childhood environments.

Educational leaders must use their training to collaborate with teachers, parents, and community members to advocate for individual students. I created a special "Getting to Know Your Child Questionnaire" to facilitate parent communication. It's really eight basic questions. Educators use this, as appropriate, to honor parents' essential role. This school-based conversation between parent and child, shared with educators can provide a critical building block for the most important factor of success – ***RELATIONSHIPS.***

You have full permission to use this communication tool, as appropriate.

GETTING TO KNOW YOUR CHILD QUESTIONNAIRE

Dear Parent/Guardian,

Please fill out the following questionnaire and return it to school with your child tomorrow.

1. Child's Name: ______________________________
   Birthday: ______________
2. I'd describe my child as:
3. One important thing for you to know about my child is:
4. What does your child like best about school?
5. What are some of your child's strengths?
6. List some of the activities of most interest to your child.
7. What hopes, or goals do you have for your child in this grade?
8. Other comments

Signed _______________________ Date:______

CUESTIONARIO PARA CONOCER MEJOR A SU NIÑO

Estimado Padre/Encargado,

Favor de llenar el siguiente cuestionario y regréselo a la escuela con su niño(a) mañana.

1. Nombre del niño(a): ______________________________
   Fecha de nacimiento ______

2. Describiría a mi niño como:

3. Una cosa importante que debe saber acerca de mi niño(a) es:

4. ¿Qué es lo que más le gusta a su niño de su escuela?

5. ¿Cuáles son las áreas fuertes de su niño(a)?

6. Enumere algunas de las actividades que más le interesan a su niño(a).

7.¿Qué deseos o metas tiene usted para su hijo(a) en este grado?

8. ¿Comentarios adicionales?

Firma ___________________________ Fecha_______

COMMUNICATING SPECIAL NEEDS NEED TO KNOW VS. CONFIDENTIALITY

There are times when students have special needs that must be communicated while guarding confidentiality. In reviewing hundreds of completed parent questionnaires, numerous special considerations for students with and without formal Individual Education Plans (IEPs) were noted.

This is critical information that must be shared on a "need to know" basis. There can be ethical, and in the cases of IEPs compliance, legal considerations. Lack of critical information has resulted in tragic consequences. I had a student without an IEP react violently to a comment from a teacher who was unaware of a family situation. The student was a sixteen-year-old, six-foot-tall high school freshman with a bad habit of using foul language in his regular conversation. When the teacher tried to lighten the situation by saying "Didn't your mother teach you not to use that kind of language in mixed company?" the student reacted violently. So much so, that the teacher sought administrative assistance and protection.

I arranged for the teacher to be in a safe setting and secured the student. In interviewing him, he was relatively calm saying "My mother's name should not be coming out of his (the teacher's) mouth like that!" He also added that he liked the teacher and never had any kind of issue with him in the past.

He had a ***reason*** for his actions but not an ***excuse!*** The back-story was that this student was given up at birth by his birth mother due to her drug involvement. She had recently addressed her demons and was reconciled with her son. They were getting to know each other after all those years.

When the teacher asked, "Didn't your mother teach you not to use that kind of language in mixed company?" the answer is really, no, she didn't. He was just getting to know her. The relationship was still raw and new. While the teacher did not need to know all of the details of this situation, he did need to know that mentioning this student's family was very sensitive, and best to avoid.

A very different case involved an upper elementary school student with an IEP who exhibited angry outbursts. Teachers needed to know how the situation was being addressed, to guide their interventions. In this case, both parents were physicians who had their child in intensive treatment to address these outbursts. Progress was being made and behavior triggers had been identified. The teachers needed to know this important information regarding the appropriate interventions, but not the details about the student's medical treatments.

To address these, and numerous other situations, I developed a special "Student Engagement Sheet (SES)." It is really an individualized menu of actions and interventions shared with educators on a need-to-know basis. Here is a sample:

YOUR SCHOOL LETTERHEAD

CONFIDENTIAL CONFIDENTIAL CONFIDENTIAL CONFIDENTIAL

Open Window of Engagement
Student Engagement Sheet (SES)

Colleagues

We all strive to improve communications and student engagement. There are times where students have different needs and show us different windows to engagement. Please consider the following accommodations for the student listed below for the time period indicated. This information is confidential. *Your Administrative Team*

Student: ________________ **Time Period:** __________

Difficulty controlling certain behaviors may not be the result of an individual's willful disobedience or defiance. While his parents are investigating all options and underlying causes, all classroom teachers who work with ________________ should consider providing the supports listed below:

- Additional time to complete assignments, gather materials, and orient during transitions.
- Monitor to help distinguish between information that is essential and information that is not.

- Simple, clear, and concise language, spoken at a slow, deliberate pace is likely to help.
- Where possible, provide scheduling consistency and avoid sudden changes.
- Prepare him for change whenever possible; tell student about assemblies, fire drills, guest speakers, and testing schedules.
- Use frequent check-ins to monitor progress and stress.
- Find opportunities throughout the day to comment on what the student did right.
- Tantrums or meltdowns (terms that are often used interchangeably) have lessened in recent years. Most meltdowns do not occur without warning. There is often a pattern of behavior, which is sometimes subtle, that suggests an imminent, behavioral outburst. Prevention through the use of appropriate academic, environmental, social, and sensory supports, as well as modification to environment and expectations, are the most effective methods.
- Avoid comments about family.
- Avoid loud speaking.
- Pronoun choice

Parent/Guardian Conference date ______________________

YOUR SCHOOL LETTERHEAD/MISSION

This sample displays a menu of suggested interventions. In actual use, just those appropriate for the student are included in their SES notifications. You have permission to use this SES form and procedure as appropriate.

CLASSROOM MANAGEMENT THAT WORKS.

Oftentimes educational leaders must intervene in academic situations. Teachers and students sometimes clash in unhealthy ways that relate to classroom management techniques. When teachers get frustrated, things can deteriorate quickly. Students and teachers get stuck in power struggles. You can guess who usually "wins."

You can help teachers who need classroom management tips by sharing the Management Involvement Feedback Focus (MIFF) techniques. Please review these enjoyable strategies, and feel free to share them. The source is a wonderful math guru, **Tom Lester**. I had the pleasure of attending several of his "***Math Matters***" workshops over the years.

Here are MIFF Technique suggestions that have been used very effectively:

MANAGEMENT INVOLVEMENT FEEDBACK FOCUS (MIFF)

1. **Hand and Finger Signals**
   Hand and Finger signals are used to allow students a consistent way of responding. Whether it be raising your hand or waving arms across each other to show disagreement, these silent modes allow everyone to participate without distracting from the lesson.

   Silent Agreement: thumbs up

   Silent Disagreement: arms & hands waved across each other (Note: also known as the "I have another answer" signal)

   "I don't know" or "I'm confused": hand moving back and forth over head

   "I can't hear": hand behind ear

   "I have an important question off the subject": raised pinky finger

The sign for "bathroom" is made by forming the right hand into the letter "t." The palm side is facing away from you. Shake your hand side to side a couple times. Some people use a twisting movement instead of the side-to-side shake. Either is fine.

2. **Space**
   The use of space in the classroom is important for a variety of reasons. A teacher must use the full space of the classroom to facilitate the active involvement of as many children as possible. As one proceeds through a lesson, one moves to various parts of the room. The goal is to use space to bring about desired behaviors such as on task behavior (move in close), louder speech (move to the other side of the room, hand behind ear), increased participation (teacher stands in back, students present at board).

3. **Modes of Response** (<u>A favorite strategy when teachers have difficulty with students shouting out</u>)
   If a mode of response is given before a question is asked, students will not have to try to guess how they should respond. When there is not a mode of response given, one or more students will have called out an answer while other students are trying to guess what kind of response was expected.
   Examples:
   I'll take a quiet hand...
   Show me on your fingers...

Whisper to your neighbor...
Talk it over in your group...
Write on your paper...

4. **Specific Questions**
   In class, it would be ideal if students never had to guess at what a teacher was asking, yet often, teachers ask questions which are vague, but in the teacher's mind require a specific answer. If the question posed is not specific, but a specific answer is wanted, then this is a head trip. Teachers should try to avoid playing this game by phrasing their questions carefully. There are times when open questions should be asked, but one must be aware of what type of question has been asked. If a question has been inadvertently open to interpretation, student thinking needs to be honored, even if the answer is not the one expected.

5. **Circulation**
   While students are working in groups or independently, the teacher has an excellent opportunity to move among students, looking and listening, asking questions to find out about student thinking or extend it, and give hints. This provides a quick assessment and often the chance to intervene on the spot.

6. **Positive Reinforcement**
   Positive Reinforcement of Behavior
   When specific desired behaviors are acknowledged by the teacher, it both informs and motivates students. For example, "I see that group 3 has put down their pencils and they all have their eyes on me."
   Positive Reinforcement of Answer
   It could be said that there are no wrong answers, we just have to find the question the student answered. For instance, "That would be right if I'd asked for the sum of 5 and 2, but I am looking for the product of 5 and 2."

7. **No Echo**
   Often teachers can slip into the habit of automatically repeating everything any student says. As a habit, echoing student responses can have several negative impacts in the classroom. If the teacher repeats everything, students will know that they don't have to listen to each other if it's important, the teacher will repeat it. A great deal of rich dialogue among students is lost this way, and students are likely to have a more difficult time working in groups because they are not in the habit of respecting what each person has to say. Some examples of alternatives to echoing are:
   "Would you please repeat your answer, but first let me go over to the opposite side of the room."
   "Raise your hand if you heard Peter."
   "If you heard it, whisper it to a neighbor who didn't hear it."
   "How many understood Martha's answer?"
   "Who can give another explanation in their own words?"

8. **Wait Time**
   A well established management technique is to allow students time to digest a question and think through an answer, it is included here because it is so powerful in the classroom. It is recommended that 3-5 seconds are allowed to pass between a question and asking for a response.

9. **Deliberate Misteaks**
   Deliberate Misteaks can be a wonderful way to assess student understanding and increase student focus on the lesson. When students are comfortable with knowledge, they love to show what they know and catch the teacher at a mistake. Not to be used while developing concepts.

10. **Involvement of Visitors**
    In order to reduce the distraction of the arrival of a visitor in the classroom, the visitor might be asked to call on a quiet hand. Or the visitor might be invited to look at some

of the students' work and find an answer or an approach that is notable. Students come to see visitors as part of the classroom experience.

FOCUS THEIR ATTENTION FOCUS TECHNIQUE

Why use them?

- To get the students' attention. *
- To maximize instructional time and minimize time wasted during transitions.
- To review important math vocabulary and concepts.

Examples

Use this list as a springboard to get started. This list is not grade level specific, but it is leveled from easier to harder examples. Start each one by saying, "If you can hear my voice, please..."

- Clap the # of sides on a ___(geometric shape).
- Show me on your fingers (SMOYF) the # of ___(sides, vertices, edges, faces, angles) on a ___ (geometric figure)
- SMOYF the # of cents in a ___(penny, nickel, dime).
- SMOYF ___ (1 more, 1 less, 2 more, 2 less) than ___(any #).
- SMOYF ___ (1,2,3...) more / less than the # I'm showing you (you hold up a # on your fingers).
- SMOYF the ___(sum, difference, product) of ___ and ___ (include negative #'s for grades 4-6).
- Make a ___(right, acute, obtuse) angle with your arm.
- When I count to 3, please tell me the # of degrees in a right angle.
- Make a polygon with your fingers.
- SMOYF the ___(1st, 2nd, 3rd...) odd number.
- SMOYF the ___(1st, 2nd, 3rd...) even number.
- SMOYF the digit in the ___ place in the # written on the board.
- SMOYF the # of feet in a yard.

- SMOYF the # inches in half a foot.
- Tell me the # of ___(in., ft., mm., cm.) in a ___(ft., yd., cm., m.).
- SMOYF ___(1/2, 1/3, 2/3, 3/6,) of ___(any #).
- Show me a ___(horizontal, vertical) line with your arm.
- Show me parallel lines with your arms.
- Show me intersecting lines with your arms.
- Show me the direction of the ___(x or y) axis with your arm.
- Show me the square root of ___ (4, 9, 16, 25, 36, 49. 64. 81, 100) on your fingers.
- SMOYF the # of factors a prime # has.
- SMOYF the ___(1st, 2nd,) prime #.
- SM OYF ___10%, 20%, etc.) of ___(any #)
- (Have data on the board or smart board) SMOYF the _(range, mode, median, mean) of the set

*I have used the focus technique to get the attention of adult groups prior to addressing them. Usually, I will ask them to Show Me On Your Fingers (SMOYF) the square root of four... or SMOYF one plus one. It works so much better than other attention-getting techniques that are less respectful.

DESIGNING CLASSROOM LESSONS

There are times when educational leaders must roll up their sleeves and directly support teachers in their lesson design and reflection efforts. Strategic, thoughtful lessons are essential to classroom and schoolwide culture. The "**Core Issues of Lesson Design and Reflection,**" is credited to the University of Pittsburgh, Institute for Learning (IFL). When used with fidelity these fifteen questions help produce intentionally enjoyable lessons for students and their teachers. Here is a listing of the questions:

CORE ISSUES OF LESSON DESIGN AND REFLECTION

WHAT?

1. *What is the intended student learning? What are the skills, concepts, habits of mind being developed? (***Students will learn __________so they can do __________***.)*
2. *To what standard(s) is the lesson content connected?*
3. *What difficulties, misunderstandings, or misconceptions might students have about this content?*
4. *What theories of teaching and learning support this lesson design?*

HOW?

5. *How will the teacher model/explain clear expectations for the students' learning?*
6. *How will each activity promote rigorous thinking?*
7. *How will students be grouped for learning? How is the grouping related to the lesson content?*
8. *How will accountable student talk and collaboration be encouraged in an atmosphere of mutual respect?*
9. *How will students make public their thinking and learning?*
10. *How will assistance be provided to individual students (Struggling students as well as those needing an extra challenge)?*
11. *How will student learning be assessed by the teacher and by the students themselves?*
12. *How will student accomplishment be recognized?*
13. *How will the teacher do things differently the next time? How will instruction proceed from here?*

WHY?

14. *Why is the lesson content appropriate to the students' spiritual and academic learning needs and prior knowledge?*
15. *Why are these instructional strategies/learning activities appropriate to the lesson goals?*

Adapted from the University of Pittsburgh – Institute for Learning

One of my favorite teachers, Charlie Mojkowski, teamed with his former student Elliot Washor to publish a wonderful book titled, "***Leaving to Learn, How Out-of-School Learning Increases Student Engagement and Reduces Dropout Rates.***" He addresses the deeper meanings why young people disengage from school. He says, "It's an alarming fact: in the U.S., one student drops out of school every 12 seconds… Our goal is not merely to graduate every student but to prepare graduates who are uncommonly ready for success in their workplaces and their communities."

The "Big Four" reasons young people disengage from school are: academic failure, behavior, life events, and disinterest. The "Deeper Four" according to Mojkowski and Washor are: not mattering, not fitting in, unrecognized talents and interests, and restrictions. When young people find that they do not matter in school and cannot find a way to fit in, they look for other places to satisfy their need to learn and succeed. They ask, "Does the school care about my interests or who I am? What if I learn, look, or sound different? How can educators address these needs?

A very simple exercise helped me nurture relationships directly with students. Prior to each class, I asked students to state (in writing) five things that are important to them right now, and five things that they think will be important to them at least ten years from now. Some of the future things are required to be different from the current ones.

WHAT IS IMPORTANT TO YOU? THE 5 THINGS HANDOUT

Name: ______________________________ Date: ______________

Name five things that are very important to you right now.

1. ____

2. ____

3. ____

4. ____

5. ____

Name five things that will be very important to you in the future (at least 10 years from now) – some things should be different.

1. ____

2. ____

3. ____

4. ____

5. ____

This simple exercise has yielded amazing insights that were needed to build relationships with students.

TEACHERS THAT SOUND LIKE ME

"To have another language is to possess a second soul."
Charlemagne

There is a special initiative that has the potential to help build relationships within diverse communities. The ***"Teachers That Sound Like Me!" Initiative.***

Having educators that look like the students they teach is a highly valued characteristic. This can involve a long-range strategy. It is also something that is beyond the control of the current staff. People can't change their race or national origin. They should not be disadvantaged by this factor that is clearly beyond their control.

There is a healthy, equitable, strategy to increase diverse perspectives and student connections with their teachers that can be open to all teachers and administrators regardless of race or national origin – ***"Teachers That Sound Like Me!"*** In one of my inner-city schools, the students were from many different countries and cultures, a very large percentage of them spoke Spanish. A little more than forty percent of the parents spoke a language other than English at home. Teachers and administrators who made the effort to gain proficiency in their students' home languages experienced wonderful, enhanced connections.

Educational leadership giants must bring this ***"Teachers That Sound Like Me!"*** initiative to scale in their school communities. Multiple language proficiency should be treated like the advanced degree stipends in many collective bargaining agreements. Language proficiency can be measured by the **American Council on the Teaching of Foreign Languages (ACTFL)** standards. Using bi-lingual students as instructors in this program adds another dimension to this initiative. Honoring their language proficiency and having them serve as teachers to their teachers yields amazing results. It is personalization at a very special level.

SUPPORTING MILITARY STUDENTS AND THEIR FAMILIES

I worked with an outstanding superintendent who was a retired Army Colonel. He encouraged my efforts to support military families. There are currently more than 2 million uniformed service members and 2.6 million military family members across the globe. In addition to recognizing their service and sacrifices, educational leaders must address some of the special considerations needed.

I was trained through The **Military Child Education Coalition**, and I am grateful for the input on this topic of the following organizations: **Virginia Joint Military Family Services Board; Family Support Center – Langley Air Force Base, Virginia; Army Community Services – Fort Eustis, Virginia; Coast Guard Family Program – Portsmouth, Virginia; Navy Family Service Centers of Hampton Roads, Hampton Roads, Virginia**; and the guidance of **Colonel Andre Thibeault.**

The military remains a mystery to many civilians. The special language, dress, titles, and traditions can be overwhelming. Military families do not want to be singled out for special attention. However, it is helpful for educators to have a basic understanding of issues impacting the lifestyle of military families.

What follows is some basic information about the armed forces and the many resources available to improve the quality of life for these special members of our learning community *Beyond the Yellow Ribbon.*

RESERVES

Reserve soldiers perform only part-time duties as opposed to full-time ("active duty") soldiers but rotate through mobilizations to full-time duty. When not on active duty, reserve soldiers typically perform training or service one weekend per month (inactive duty for training or "Battle Assembly") and for two continuous weeks at some time during the year (annual training).

Branches of the armed services have different missions, and these differences often account for differences in family life. The mission of one branch of the service may require short, frequent separations while another branch might require longer, less frequent separations. These different patterns of separation can require different adjustments on the part of family members. Separations and deployments are a fact of life for all military families.

There are four main aspects of military life – deployment, reunion, crisis, and relocation. They will be examined as they relate to military children.

THE DEPLOYMENT CYCLE

Pre-deployment →Deployment →Reunion → Equilibrium →

Deployments or separations are faced by all military families at some time in their careers. The frequency and duration of these separations may vary depending on the branch of the service or the service member's job, but many of the emotional issues military families face are the same.

Healthy families share many characteristics: adaptability, flexibility, and clarity of family rules are some of the most important. For military families these strengths are critical. Some refer to them as "accordion families." They stretch out and expand to let the service member in after a deployment, and they compress and condense when the member deploys. This astonishing feat might not be accomplished without help from outside the family.

Many individuals currently serving in the armed forces were raised in military families and chose a military career because they had positive experiences as military children. One group of public-school teachers was quoted as saying that when the right supports are given, "... military students are culturally and politically aware, good team players, and independent, self-reliant, reach out to newcomers easily, and make good world citizens."

Although the frequency and duration of these separations may vary depending on the branch of the service or the service member's job, many of the emotional issues military families face are the same. Some common Emotional Signs of Deployment Stress cited by the Military Child Education Coalition include anger, grief, numbness, sadness, feelings of abandonment, isolation/loneliness, fear/worry, sense of betrayal, denial, low self-esteem, depression, loss of stability, and confusion.

Some deployment stressors and common behavioral (generalized) signs may include uncontrollable crying, separation anxiety, withdrawal/overly quiet, disorientation/recklessness, sleep difficulties, eating difficulties, acting out at home & school, loss of control, misdirected anger, self-criticism, loss of interest, hurt self, others, pets, intentionally, discontinued care of personal appearance, possible drug & alcohol abuse, regressive behavior, lying/cover up, risky sexual behavior.

Sudden deployments can cause additional stress. Coast Guard members respond to coastal emergencies i.e., search and rescue, pollution control, port security. They may have no return date. The family can't use the countdown calendar etc.).

Hazardous duty brings great stress. Military families routinely deal with the possibility of their loved ones being killed or severely injured. Insensitive media coverage, including improper notice of publication can add to the stress.

Young children may not fully understand the reasons behind the service member's departure. In their minds, they may be choosing to go away. They may feel abandoned or feel the service member is going away because of something they did. They may feel guilty. Teenagers may feel resentment toward the service member or a desire to take the parent's place, as well as guilt for those feelings.

Sensing a loss of continuity, children may continually "test" behavioral boundaries. This is similar to the reactions of some children of divorce. They worry about what will happen to them. Will the non-deployed parent leave, too? (If the parent is supported in maintaining a positive attitude and models effective coping skills, most likely the child will do the same.

Educational leaders can assist military children and their parents in the following ways: Referring to military family support organizations, especially – www.militaryonesource.com is a great one. It encourages military parents to provide the school with the name of the unit they are assigned to and when the unit deploys.

This helps educators to be attuned to any emotional, behavioral, or academic changes that may occur with a student as a result of deployment. It also encourages regular communication with deployed parents (pen pals?). Military parents should visit their children's teachers to make them aware. Deployment support groups can be exceptionally helpful.

Homecoming of a service member is a time of celebration and change. The weeks and days before homecoming are filled with mounting excitement, tension, and nervousness. Days may be spent in preparation. Fantasies of an even better relationship may surface and take the place of reality as the day of homecoming draws closer. There is a period of readjustment and increased tension as the idealized relationship confronts reality.

Families often comment about homecoming strengths. They take the opportunity to evaluate the changes that have occurred in the family, to determine the future direction of this growth, and to experience renewed and refreshed family relationships. They may be less likely to take each other for granted. Children may learn about adjusting, renegotiating roles, accepting change, and developing new skills.

Relocation is a major concern. The average American family moves once every five years. For some military families this figure can escalate to relocation every two years, twice the national average. A career in the military could result in ten to twelve relocations. Military members have limited ability to choose where their next duty station will be, and subsequently how this will affect their families' lifestyle, job opportunities, education, and friendships.

As with homecoming, relocation can have a positive impact. Career advancement may be involved. Meeting new people and broadening cultural horizons can be very beneficial. Military children tend to be culturally aware and knowledgeable in geography and social studies, independent, self-reliant, and better "team players."

Essential to serving in the military, and indeed all students is taking a **personalized approach** to education.

"***Some say that we can't afford to personalize education to all students. The truth is that we can't afford not to***".
Mojkowski and Washor

Leaders must honor the high expectations students have for their schools regarding relationships, relevance, authenticity, and application.

- Relationships: Do my teachers and others who might serve as my teachers know about me and my interests and talents?
- Relevance: Do I find what the school is teaching relevant to my interests?
- Authenticity: Is the learning and work I do regarded as significant outside school by my communities of practice and by experts, family, and employers?
- Application: Do I have opportunities to apply what I am learning in real world settings and contexts?

Students who feel connected to their school are, as adults, less likely to have emotional distress, suicidal ideation, physical violence victimization or perpetration, multiple sex partners, sexually transmitted diseases, prescription drug misuse or illicit-drug use.

There is a tremendous gap between mental health services needed and mental health services received. Nearly 59% of adolescents ages 12–17 with a major depressive episode did not receive any type of treatment. The service gap is even larger among young people of color. Hispanic and black adolescents were less likely than their white peers to receive services for mood and anxiety disorders, even when these disorders were associated with severe impairment.

EDUCATIONAL LEADERS MUST ELEVATE AND INTEGRATE MENTAL HEALTH EDUCATION INTO THE SCHOOL ENVIRONMENT.

Much of this work is the turf of the professional school counselor. The American School Counselor Association (ASCA) suggests that historically, the term "guidance counselor" was used to refer to counselors working in the schools. This term has evolved to "school counselor" as the scope of duties has changed and evolved. Although some schools still use the "guidance counselor" term, the American School Counselor Association (ASCA) encourages the use of "school counselor" to reflect the role more accurately. I find myself using the outdated guidance counselor term for clarity in many situations. (*I thank my college graduate program director, and former ASCA President, for her patience on this.)*

Supervisory Educational Leaders are often called to assess and support the work of their professional school counselors. They often ask me for guidance in these efforts. In a comprehensive, collaborative process, counselors need to report out not only **what** they do, but also the **results** of what they do! I developed a "Counselor Activity Report" for this process (see below). It is aligned to the ASCA model categories of Academic, Personal Social, Careers. It also records the results data from the counseling activities. I used these data points to advocate for the counselors I supervised. As a result of these initiatives and protocols, many school counseling positions were saved – which benefited many students.

COUNSELOR REPORT

Academic – General	Q 1	Q 2	Q 3	Q 4	YTD
Daily Reports					
New Student Orientations					
Enrollments/Withdrawals					
Special Populations Meetings – IEP / ELL / 504					
Meetings with School Administration					
Meetings with Parents					
Meetings with Teachers					
Testing / Placement					
ILP Meetings					
Parent Letters					
Parent Phone Calls/ emails/texts					
Students Needing Homework Help					
Students Counseled Regarding MS Transition					
Students in Danger of Failing a Course					
Students Referred for ELA Tutoring					
Number of Advisory Sessions Supported					
Students Referred for Math Tutoring					

Academic – Secondary	Q 1	Q 2	Q 3	Q 4	YTD
Letters of Recommendation					
Transcripts & Graduation Requirement Review					
SAT info, registration, IDs, preparation					
College Counseling & Research with Students					
Financial Aid Night & FASFA					
College Applications – Number of Students					
College Scholarship Money Awarded					
College Acceptances					
College Financial Aid Packages Reviewed					
Credit Audits					
Advanced Placement – General					
Students Who Know About AP Courses					
Number of Students Identified HS Choices					
Students Counseled Regarding HS Transition					
Credit Recovery Placements					
Schedule Changes (L! Test / Place, Overages)					
Academic: Other					

Emotional / Personal / Social	Q 1	Q 2	Q 3	Q 4	YTD
Daily Reports – Emotional / Personal / Social					
Discipline Referral / Mediation Meetings					
Critical / Dangerous / Safety – Counsel Referrals					
Students Who Needed Conflict Resolution					
DCYF / Outside Agency Calls					
Students in Mortal Danger					
Students Hospitalized					
Substance Issues – Counseling and Referrals					
Bullying / Harassment / Texting / Sexting					
Meetings: Outside Agencies					

Emotional / Personal / Social	Q 1	Q 2	Q 3	Q 4	YTD
Attendance – Transportation Issues					
Attendance – A-8's and Truancy					
Attendance – Phone Calls and Conferences					
Community Service: In-School (Tutor & Other)					
Social & Interpersonal R/S Counseling					
Focus: Students Referred for the First Time					
Focus: Students Referred for Different Offense					
Focus: Calls to Administration from Focus					
Focus: Students Referred for the Same Offense					
Focus: Students in Danger of Failing a Course					

Career	Q 1	Q 2	Q 3	Q 4	YTD
Career Interest Inventory Completed					
Students Who have Identified Career Study					
Drivers Education Process					

Career	Q 1	Q 2	Q 3	Q 4	YTD
Meetings with Students – Grad. Requirements					
Students with Job Placement Assistance					
Community Service: Outside Services					

LEADERS PROMOTING DISCIPLINE STRATEGIES THAT WORK AT HOME AND AT SCHOOL

The major contributors to my thinking and field use of discipline strategies that work, are **Dr. Ivan Fitzwater,** and **Professor Ralph Montella**. I participated in many workshops with Dr. Fitzwater and enjoyed his homespun sense of humor and traditional insights. Professor Montella is a lifelong friend and I consider him a mentor. I mentioned him earlier in the comment about looking deeper into student behaviors and the ***$10,000 pom-pom***.

As a school psychologist and educational leadership expert he has guided and supported countless teachers, administrators, and counselors. I cherish the numerous classes and workshops he facilitated and his continued support and advice.

Dr. Fitzwater wrote many books, poems, and other publications. One of my favorites is his poem, "Only a teacher." I share it here:

Only a Teacher
By Ivan Fitzwater
I am a teacher!

What I do and say are being absorbed by young minds
who echo those images across the ages.
My lessons will be immortal,
affecting people yet unborn,
people I will never see or know.
The future of the world is in my classroom today-
a future with the potential for good or bad.
The pliable minds of tomorrow's leaders will be molded
either artistically or grotesquely by what I do.

Several future presidents are learning from me today-
so are the great writers of the next decades
and so are the so-called ordinary people
who make the decisions in a democracy.
I must never forget these same people
could be the thieves and murderers of the future.

Only a teacher.
Thank God I have a calling to the greatest
profession of all.
I must be vigilant every day
lest I lose one fragile opportunity
to improve tomorrow.

This serves as a springboard for a critical, and often misunderstood aspect of school and home life – ***DISCIPLINE.***

What is Discipline? Steps, policies, or actions we implement to help our children succeed academically and socially. We see in this definition not only what is stated, but also what is NOT stated. There is no mention of punishment. As a principal, I enjoyed and encouraged it when I was described as "strict, but not mean!"

Clear behavioral expectations are critical. There are numerous debates about the value of extrinsic rewards for behaviors.

One of my first experiences in transitioning from a business professional to an educator involved visiting a middle school with someone who motivated me to enter the profession.

Joe Maguire was a gifted school administrator, generous, kind, and a forceful human being. He invited me to spend a full day shadowing him. The key was how he connected with students. Regarding rewards, I saw him do something that I borrowed many times as a principal. As we walked the corridors of the school, a student reached down and picked up a discarded paper. When Joe saw this, he reached into his pocket and gave the student a dollar! Other students saw this and were clearly impressed. They started picking up papers that they "found" on the ground and showing them to Joe, expecting their dollar. Joe calmly stated "Cleaning up your school is great...Thank you! But you never know when I might give someone a dollar for doing it!"

When rewards are somewhat random it can be an important step in increasing rather than harming intrinsic motivation. Other steps can include setting and communicating behavior goals that are achievable and measurable, defining how you will use the random reward system, and explaining why a random reward is given. When people (children and adults) feel that you value and care for them as individuals, they are more willing to comply with your wishes. Strategies to show you care include sincere listening, taking the time to teach and enforce acceptable behavior, and showing an interest in their beliefs. Remember, one of the best gifts you can give someone is your undivided attention. If your phone or other device screen is visible to them during your conversations, it limits the perceived level of your attention.

Do you know what is important to the person you are trying to influence? Be intentional about learning what is important to them. The "5 Things Handout" I shared earlier is a start, as is the "Getting to Know Your Child Questionnaire." These are not "one and done" exercises. Follow up is essential. I asked a group of 6 students that were part of our inner-city District Wide Student Government (DWSG) the "5 Things" questions. This is one of the few times I invited a group response. Think about how their responses would guide your own follow-up educational supports.

For currently important things as a group they said, Family, Grades, Friends, Phone, and Money. For the future they ranked Family, Career/job, Money (car – blue BMW), Continuing education (law school Harvard). The follow-up for these students included intentional additional outreach to their families, career interest inventory work (the Self-Directed Search®) and targeting college admissions and scholarship opportunities that included Ivy League institutions.

Human connection, and especially supervisory relationships often involve criticism. Constructive criticism is a wonderful gift, especially when correcting unacceptable behavior. The goals should involve reflection, genuine sorrow in the disappointment, and intentional commitment to make better choices in the future. When correcting students, allow them to keep their dignity. The correction process will be counterproductive if individuals are corrected in a manner that communicates bitterness, sarcasm, low expectations, or disgust. The goal is to provide a quick, fair, and meaningful consequence while at the same time communicating that you care for and respect the student.

Student fights are awful on so many levels. There must be no tolerance for violence. Unfortunately, many educators may need to deal with these situations. I had to intervene in one hundred eight (108) fights. (Yes, I kept count!). They were all traumatic events. Some have a way of haunting my thoughts. Students all had reasons for their actions, but never reasonable excuses.

I interviewed two young ladies after a terrible fight. Both of them were pregnant by the same young man (also a student I knew). When I asked if they were fighting over him, they both answered in unison – "He's not worth it!" Years later I ran into one of them in a parent conference in one of my schools. She was a proud young parent and her son had won an award. I recognized his strong resemblance to his father. Unfortunately, he was murdered shortly after his son was born.

In another fight involving two female students from the same extended family, they mentioned a long simmering family feud as the reason for their fight. This was not a sudden flash of emotions. The fight was planned. One of the young ladies actually had a concealed knife in her underwear that fell out during the scuffle (see picture). No serious injuries resulted in this case, but that was not always the case.

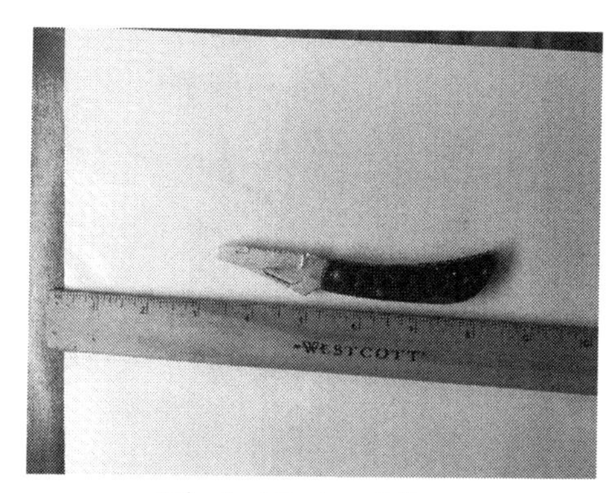

The knife that fell out

I felt obliged to protect the students by physically intervening. As a leader, I never wanted or expected other educators to put themselves in imminent danger by taking similar physical intervention actions. I have witnessed these situations result in life changing, and sometimes tragic results for the students and the educators.

My strategy was to get between the combatants and get them as far away from each other as possible. I relied more on my martial arts training and advice from self-defense experts to **block, protect, and separate** the combatants. Calm, but firm verbal commands accompanied the separation and de-escalation efforts.

Follow up is very dependent on the clear expectations and communication of policies. In a physical confrontation, self-defense typically allows a person who reasonably believes he is about to be hit to defend himself. However, if you've already been hit, and the person who hit you indicates by words or actions that he is not going to hit you again, self-defense generally does not allow you to hit that person back. Self-defense may only be invoked to prevent further harm, not to retaliate against a person who has already harmed you.

Outside the home, a person is generally expected to retreat before using deadly force in self-defense. Remember the important guidelines on personal safety versus self-defense. There should be comprehensive, strategic personal safety guidelines and practices in place that limit, and hopefully eliminate the need for self-defense action. In schools, a positive relationship between parents and teachers is a great asset in creating a safer, and healthier culture.

PARENT/TEACHER CONFERENCES – BEST PRACTICES

Parent/Teacher Conferences are great opportunities to enhance relationships. There are a few basics that may help. The solution-focused goal is to improve and facilitate the relationship. Wherever possible start the conference with the child out of the room; especially if there may be some areas of disagreement. Avoid discussing family problems, other teachers, comparisons to siblings, arguing in front of the child, or blaming misbehavior on others.

The focus must quickly transition from the problem to the positive solutions. End the conference in a hopeful tone. What has worked before in addressing this challenge? Summarize the main points discussed and any steps to be taken. Follow up with notes, email, texts, or a phone call, especially if a particular positive strategy has been identified for attention.

DISCIPLINE FOR STUDENTS WITH SPECIAL NEEDS

There are specific interventions for students with special needs that are especially appropriate for those with diagnosed conditions. I have found that many of these strategies are helpful with all students. For a student to be diagnosed as having Oppositional Defiant Disorder (ODD), that student must have had an official assessment that involves a team of professionals. There are a number of misconceptions or "myths" regarding interventions. Here is a partial listing:

ODD Myths vs. Reality

- Myth – ignore behavior.
    - Reality- impulse driven – ignoring →no effect.
- Myth – harsh punishment
    - Reality- punishment means little.
- Myth – they need idle time.
    - Reality – better behaved when active and task-oriented.
- Myth – surprises and sudden changes motivate.
    - Reality – structure, order, consistency is needed.
- Myth – Threats intimidate.
    - Reality – creates more defiance.
- Myth – Praise motivates children with ODD.
    - Reality – Children with ODD may perceive praise as manipulation and control.

Similarly, there are positive teacher classroom strategies to improve connection to students with ODD:

- Use the Student Engagement Sheet to inform specific interventions with the student.
- Make intentional efforts to improve students' damaged self-esteem - People respond to gentleness.
- Give students choices – from a menu of positive, healthy choices.
- Set up clear classroom parameters that are firm, fair, and consistent.
- Get/keep the parent involved.
- Make expectations very clear – FOLLOW THROUGH
- Without a positive relationship between student and teacher, little collaboration is possible.
- Teachers should never lose supervisory contact with their students – No sending out!
  - While there are times for teachers and students to disengage from a conflict, students should never be sent out of a classroom unsupervised. There must always be a chain of custody/responsibility for the student. As an administrator, my teachers always had access to me (or a designee) as an emergency student pick up to defuse a classroom situation.
  - Unsupervised students with special needs are often a danger to themselves and to others. I have intervened for unsupervised "sent-out" students who were disrupting other classes, causing emergency situations, and sometimes leaving the school building. There was one memorable case where a "sent-out" student climbed into the dropped ceiling of a schoolroom, crawled a distance and finally fell through into another room.

Another condition impacting students is Attention Deficit/ Hyperactivity Disorder (ADHD). ADHD is one of the most common neurodevelopmental disorders of childhood. It is usually first diagnosed in childhood and often lasts into adulthood. Children with ADHD may have trouble paying attention, controlling impulsive behaviors (may act without thinking about what the result will be), or be overly active. ADHD involves about 3-5% of the school-age population (more boys). Some children without ADHD diagnosis may exhibit similar characteristics. The strategies suggested here should be considered for those students as well.

Students with ADHD may have distractibility, difficulty listening and staying on task and focused; difficulty following directions; a tendency to jump among tasks; difficulty keeping track of assignments and materials; and a tendency to be easily frustrated and overwhelmed. Management techniques are not different from other students, but more interventions and more frequent applications are needed. Directions often need to be repeated and separated into smaller steps, often called chunking. Teachers should avoid punitive measures and permissive approaches; these result in power struggles – waste of time and damage the relationship between adult and child.

Positive Classroom general conditions for the child with ADHD often include: a predictable schedule that includes regular breaks; lots of non-verbal (cuing) to help keep the flow of the lesson; assistance to help the child with organization (e.g. color code topics, subjects, etc.); immediate feedback during lessons that avoid confrontations (at all costs!); student options (all good ones); frequent positive reinforcement, and smaller student/teacher ratio.

Teachers are encouraged to make appropriate content modifications. This does NOT mean lowering standards. It is a leveling of the playing field for the individual. The student's strengths should be used. Often, exceptional visual learners with ADHD respond to instructions that are bold, colorful, simple, and Spartan. Where practical, I like to use a twenty font for printed instructions. Activities-based assignments are very effective. In times of frustration, teachers may need to step back. Having high standards does not involve expectations of perfection. Teachers that maintain a healthy sense of humor and unconditional positive regard for their students report a much higher level of job and life satisfaction.

CREATING FAMILY TEAMS TO PROMOTE SELF-DISCIPLINE.

Dr. Ivan Fitzwater and Professor Ralph Montella describe ways of creating a family team dedicated to promoting student self-discipline. The plan has three goals. 1) All behavior must build the individual, 2) all behavior must build the family, and 3) it must be solution focused. A primary principle is the system of reasonable but assured consequences, by which children understand the rules and know in advance the certain outcome of violating them.

The severity of a "consequence" has little to do with whether an act is repeated.

This is such an important concept. The key word here is *consequence*, as opposed to *punishment*. The thing that is crucial to correcting behavior is the inevitability of the consequence. Giving numerous chances, without consequences, reinforces improper behavior rather than correcting.

The greatest act of love is to never do anything for children which they can do for themselves.
People are expected to meet their own obligations without monitoring or reminders by others. The ultimate goal is self-discipline where no monitoring is necessary. If control must be external, it will break down. If school principals handle the misbehavior in a teacher's classroom rather than educating the teacher to be a disciplinarian, the stream of referrals to the office grows rather than diminishes.

Wherever possible, children should be allowed to be problem-solvers rather than having parents or educators step in prematurely. We must support, not rescue. The people we love are going to suffer pain which we could prevent, but this is done to avoid greater pain in the future.

Part of the team approach is recognizing problem ownership. Only the owner of the problem can provide the solution. Other team members listen but do not give answers. Our listening and questioning help the other person find the best answer. - What is the problem? What are my alternatives? What are the expected consequences of each choice?

TEACHER, COUNSELOR, PRINCIPAL, CENTRAL ADMINISTRATOR EVALUATIONS

ACCOUNTABILITY SHOULD HELP EDUCATORS INCREASE COMPETENCY, COMMITMENT, CREATIVITY, WORK SATISFACTION, AND MORALE.

Similar to our lessons on grading, assessments and evaluations of teachers, counselors, principals, and central administrators, must be based on clear expectations of the purposes and desired outcomes.

During my first three years as a middle school teacher, the principal visited my classroom three times for my "Formal Evaluation." I refer to them as "Drive-by Evaluations." There was a check-off list on a 5"x7" index card, rating me on my appearance, class control, and classroom organization. The process took approximately fifteen minutes.

This same form had been in use for at least twenty years. The process was a formality that complied with a one paragraph description in the Collective Bargaining Agreement (CBA) with the teachers' union. After the initial three-year period, I had "tenure." For the next five years, while there were no formal evaluations of my teaching, clearly the principal was assessing me and all of the teachers. We had many conversations in these early years where he commented on the special projects and learning experiences that I was developing with students, their families, colleagues, and community partners.

He even mentioned a situation that I thought was relatively confidential. There was a teacher located across the hallway from my classroom, who had a long history of disruptive student behaviors. One afternoon things were getting so loud in his classroom that it was difficult to hear in neighboring rooms. When I opened the door and looked into his room the students immediately rushed back to their seats and quieted down. The teacher was cowering in a corner of the room. I stayed while he regained his composure and things got back to some semblance of order.

The principal mentioned that he had purposely made room assignments to keep my room directly across from that particular teacher to help maintain control while he made the needed interventions. He was obviously communicating with students and a wide range of learning community stakeholders, in addition to observing our work informally, but purposefully.

None of these factors were reflected in the formal teacher evaluation process at the time. Thoughtful individual principals (***Educational Giants***) take a comprehensive, holistic approach to helping their teachers continuously grow and team. **Accountability should help educators increase competency, commitment, creativity, work satisfaction, and morale.**

The teacher evaluation process evolved rapidly in pursuit of accountability goals. Since commitment, work satisfaction and morale do not lend themselves to charted data recordings, they were not prominent features. Technology supported these limited views of accountability.

I reached out to my business contacts for perspectives. I sent the following inquiry to the president of one of the leading insurance companies in the nation- the same corporation that partnered with my middle school so many years ago when I just started my teaching career.

- Education struggles with performance evaluation. These struggles have harmful impact on students and educators. Education "experts" complain that close to 98% of teachers receive at least "satisfactory" ratings. Often this number reaches 100%. They see this as a major flaw in the system. They often want to include student test scores in evaluating teachers without considering the major limitations. Many times, a teacher will have a student in class for four months before standardized tests are administered (if at all!). There are numerous other challenges. How does this metric apply to teachers in content not subject to standardized testing? How does an evaluator (usually a principal, or other administrator) assess in an area outside of their expertise (foreign language, music, physical education, etc.)? The "Experts" try mightily to fit these disparate pieces into a meaningful picture with predictable results. It is like trying to measure someone's fitness by taking, body weight, height, minutes and types of exercise, diet, and rest, and combining them for a single number. Nothing meaningful comes of this!

- This leads to my questions "What would you do?" (WWYD). Or more accurately, "What does your company do to evaluate employee performance?" I know this is a very broad question.

- Any advice would be appreciated.

Thank you so much for your help with this.

Here is the reply:

> ***Hi Guy,***
>
> ***I believe there is no fixed or standard answer to this question, each organization has to figure out what is best for their mission, goals, and circumstances.***
>
> ***We try to set expectations for goals (for personal improvement and business/professional accomplishment) at the beginning of each year. We try to have regular dialogue with each individual on their progress against their goals during the year. We try to be supportive while at the same time allow them the freedom to accomplish their goals in a way that fits their work style and skills.***
>
> ***At the end of the year, we have a wrap up meeting to evaluate how we/they did on their goals during the year. The evaluation sessions are meant to be honest, straight forward, and respectful. We discuss what each individual did well and what they need to improve on.***

I hope this helps.

In a similar vein, I asked a Police Chief about the ways he evaluates his officers and leadership personnel. Although he used many of the same procedures as the insurance company, the nature of this paramilitary, strong union, organization included more limits on the process. He highlighted a unique and powerful practice that he was excited to share. **He required all of his direct-report personnel to include a professional, evidence-based, letter of reference from a peer to be included in their performance evidence packets.** These letters were written by colleagues who saw these workers in action.

I had the flexibility as a private school principal; to incorporate these peer appreciation letters into my schoolteacher evaluation process. It had a twofold objective: to strongly encourage teachers to observe each other teaching a class; and to gain their perspectives. I must admit that not all the teachers embraced this practice immediately.

It can be difficult to become accustomed to classroom visitors if it is a new practice. I participated in New England Association of Schools and Colleges (NEASC) Accreditation visits to a number of schools. One elementary school, in particular had great success in encouraging teachers to visit and watch each other teach. When teachers had a favorite lesson planned, they publicized it in the school announcements and school weekly newsletter and then they hung special toy binoculars on the outside of the door to invite all visitors. The host students were aware of this process, and there were times when whole classes went to visit and observe others.

School principals are accountable for the success of their schools. School counselors are accountable for the success of their students in academics, social emotional competencies, and career competencies. Like teachers, there are factors beyond these administrators' direct control or authority that impact their results.

As mentioned in the advice from the insurance company executive, goals for personal improvement for principals and counselors and professional accomplishments must be thoughtfully established at the beginning of the year. There must be vertical integration of goals. Teachers and counselors should be aware of their principal's goals. Principals should be aware of the goals of their supervisors in central administration, including the superintendent of schools. Their own goals should complement them. They all stream from the districtwide vision and mission-- the big picture.

The final piece of thoughtful evaluation systems that has potential to increase the competency, commitment, creativity, work satisfaction, and morale facets of accountability is the respect for student voice. As a college professor, I cherished the course evaluations that the students completed at the end of each semester. I studied them for ways to improve my practice. It was interesting to see that different students had divergent views on their learning experiences in the same class.

This helped me to pay more attention to individual needs (i.e., knowledge of students). Student voice is not restricted to college level students. Intentionally seeking student feedback on "what they like best" or what they would like to have more of in class can lead to amazing and useful feedback.

LOYALTY IN THE WORK SETTING

INTEGRITY, HONESTY, AND COMPASSION ARE EXPECTED. THAT IS DIFFERENT THAN ASSUMED LOYALTY

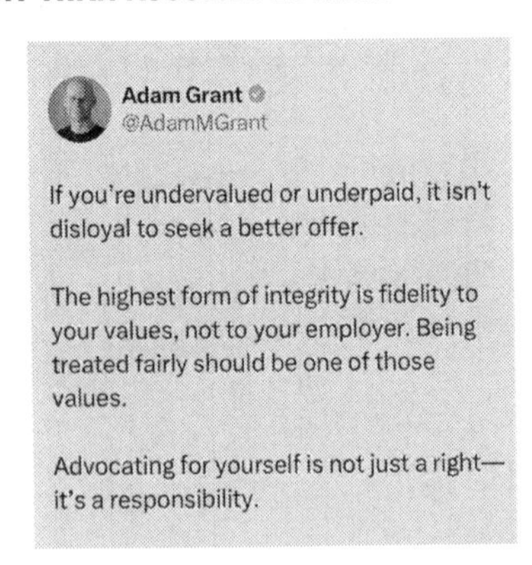

These leadership lessons started with a statement on the importance of clear expectations. Each situation that was described, had direct student benefits focus. Educational leadership is an honor and a privilege that can only be joyful when all feel appreciated. That involves what I see as clear and reasonable expectations of loyalty in the work setting.

I spent many years with the same school department and the same institution of higher education. The teams that I led and those that I supported contributed in amazing ways. They made great sacrifices to advocate for students, that I will always admire. There were times when some individuals were disappointed in the ways they were treated during their work and especially towards the end of their service. They described their lack of appreciation as acts of "disloyalty."

I saw it from a different perspective. Some of them were treated dishonestly, and some with a total lack of integrity and compassion, but **disloyalty** did not come into play. The word *loyalty* brings to mind a powerful sense of belonging and solidarity. With it comes the idea of wholehearted fidelity coupled with unswerving devotion and duty. In the Bible, the concept of loyalty is purely relational. This means our whole being is thoroughly committed to someone (Joshua 24:15).

Integrity, honesty, and compassion are noble attributes that individuals have every right to expect, **but they are different from common assumptions of loyalty**. Schools and organizations must be explicit in saying that long service will be recognized or protected, and not have it as an expected if undocumented policy. It should not be an assumption made by employees. Compassion and understanding usually aren't a part of the human resources development program. (The term human, in industry, does not imply humane.)

As Adam Grant says, "A company or school isn't a family. Parents don't fire their kids for low performance or furlough them in hard times."

When Educational Leadership Giants value the morale of their people, they are intentional in showing them integrity, honesty, and compassion. They envision their workplace as a community – a place where people bond around shared values, feel valued as human beings, and have a voice in decisions that affect them.

Now that they have been communicated, I hope that some of these lessons connected with you.

ACKNOWLEDGEMENTS

I would like to say thanks.

TO MY SUPPORT TEAM

Dave, Joe, Jodie, Jessica, Heidi, Madeline, Violet, Joshua, Andy, Lucy, Rosalina, Sam, Jameson, Tristan, Cristiano, Amy, Cassie, Chris.

TO MY MAJOR INFLUENCERS

Tim David and **Anthony Pesare,** your advice was instrumental and inspiring!

Ralph Montella, David Alba, Joseph Alba, Bill Riordan, Mary Riordan, Andy and Polly Erickson, Dan and Diane Angelone, Greg and Lisa Costantino, Russ Sabella, Javier Montanez, Mike Solitto, Tom Lester, Adam Grant, John Amaechi, Charles Mojowski, Ralph Jasparro, Mike Rose, Rick and Ann Scherza, Grandma and Grandpa Alba.

TO SOMEONE WORTHY OF EXTRA THANKS

My wonderful and patient wife, Susan J. Alba

ABOUT THE AUTHOR

Dr. Guy Alba has a B.S. In Business Management, M.Ed. in Counseling, and an Ed.D. in Educational Leadership. Prior to his work as an educator, his business career included designing athletic shoes, and owning and operating his own fitness center and karate studio. He followed his lifelong dream to become a teacher. His education work background includes teaching at the elementary, secondary, under-graduate, graduate, and adult education levels. He has served as a school counselor, elementary and secondary school principal, district wide supervisor of counseling services, and consultant/professional development facilitator at the national level. Much of his professional work has focused on facilitating school and business/community partnerships. He published the Partners Affecting Learning (PAL) Evaluation Model for School and Business Partnerships and the corresponding PAL Evaluation Tool for partnership facilitation, as well as a number of related articles. He lives in Rhode Island with his wife, Susan.

Made in the USA
Middletown, DE
07 October 2023